2013 WATCHLISTING GUIDANCE

TABLE OF CONTENTS

CHAPTER I: WATCHLISTING PROCESS AND PROCEDURES

I. INTRODUCTION

1.1 A key foundation for TERRORIST[1]-related screening is the U.S. Government's TERRORIST watchlisting process managed by the Terrorist Screening Center (TSC). The TSC was established by the Attorney General, acting through the Director of the Federal Bureau of Investigation (FBI), and in coordination with the Secretary of State, the Secretary of Homeland Security, and the then Director of Central Intelligence for the Intelligence Community (IC). The TSC is supported by the National Counterterrorism Center (NCTC), the Department of State (DOS), the Department of Homeland Security (DHS), the IC, the FBI, Law Enforcement Agencies, Regulatory Agencies and Diplomatic Bureaus. The TSC has created and maintains the Terrorist Screening Database (TSDB) or Terrorist Watchlist to serve as the U.S. Government's consolidated watchlist for TERRORISM SCREENING INFORMATION.

1.2 The current TERRORIST watchlisting process supports the U.S. Government's efforts to combat TERRORISM by: (1) consolidating the U.S. Government's Terrorist Watchlist in the TSDB; (2) helping SCREENERS and intelligence agencies accurately identify individuals on the Terrorist Watchlist; (3) providing SCREENERS with information to help them respond appropriately during ENCOUNTERS with KNOWN or SUSPECTED TERRORISTS; and, (4) subsequently collecting information about the KNOWN or SUSPECTED TERRORIST for use in assessing threats and conducting investigations.[2] The collected information may be incorporated into the Terrorist Identities Datamart Environment (TIDE) and TSDB to enhance the records of KNOWN or SUSPECTED TERRORISTS and may be made available to the wider watchlisting and screening communities. Today, the TSDB also includes information about certain foreign nationals who are associated with TERRORISM, TERRORIST ACTIVITY, or KNOWN or SUSPECTED TERRORIST(S) but for whom there is insufficient DEROGATORY INFORMATION to be independently watchlisted. This may include certain immediate family members of KNOWN or SUSPECTED TERRORISTS, or known associates of KNOWN or SUSPECTED TERRORISTS. These additional categories of records (also known as exceptions to the REASONABLE SUSPICION standard) are maintained to support immigration and screening activities primarily conducted by DOS and DHS.[3]

1.3 This Watchlisting Guidance has been developed to help standardize the watchlisting community's nomination and screening processes. It is important to remember, however, that watchlisting is not an exact science. There are inherent limitations in any primarily name-based system and analytic judgments may differ regarding whether subjective criteria have been met. Given these realities, the U.S. Government's watchlisting process attempts to safeguard the American people from a TERRORIST attack while safeguarding privacy, civil rights and civil liberties.

1.4 Thus, when reasonable minds could disagree on a record, a NOMINATOR will make a determination in favor of sending the nomination to NCTC for consideration and additional review. The TSC has the final decision authority regarding watchlisting determinations and will add an individual's name to the TSDB, consistent with TSC Actions and Processes as further described in Paragraph 1.56.

II. WATCHLISTING AUTHORITIES

1.5 On September 16, 2003, the President issued Homeland Security Presidential Directive 6 (HSPD-6), which directed the Attorney General to "establish an organization to consolidate the U.S. Government's approach to TERRORISM SCREENING and provide for the appropriate and lawful use of TERRORIST INFORMATION in screening processes."[4] TERRORIST INFORMATION was specifically defined to mean "information about individuals known or appropriately suspected to be or have been engaged in conduct constituting, in preparation for, in aid of, or related to TERRORISM." HSPD-6 also directed the heads of Executive Departments and Agencies to provide to NCTC on an on-going basis, "all appropriate TERRORIST INFORMATION in their possession, custody, or control," to the extent permitted by law.

1.6 The intent of HSPD-6 was to consolidate all TERRORISM INFORMATION at the Terrorist Threat Integration Center (TTIC) - whose functions were assumed by NCTC[5] - in a classified database that would then extract Unclassified, For Official Use Only (U//FOUO) TERRORIST IDENTIFIERS for passage to the new organization created by the Attorney General. Thus, concurrent with the issuance of HSPD-6, the TSC was established via the Memorandum of Understanding on the Integration and Use of Screening Information to Protect Against Terrorism {TSC MOU), which was signed by the Attorney General, the Secretaries of State and Homeland Security, and the Director of Central Intelligence (on behalf of the IC).[6]

1.7 Under HSPD-6, consistent with the U.S. Constitution and applicable laws, including those protecting the rights of all Americans, the TSC was to develop and maintain an unclassified database containing the most thorough, accurate, and current identity information possible about KNOWN or SUSPECTED TERRORISTS. The TSC created the TSDB to meet these goals.[7] The TSDB is also known as the Terrorist Watchlist. The TSDB receives TERRORIST IDENTIFIERS from two sources: NCTC's TIDE provides information concerning KNOWN or SUSPECTED international TERRORISTS and the TSC's Terrorist Review and Examinations Unit (TREX) provides the identities of KNOWN or SUSPECTED domestic TERRORISTS who have no link to international TERRORISM. NCTC's TIDE contains identifying and substantive DEROGATORY INFORMATION on KNOWN or SUSPECTED international TERRORISTS and the FBI's Sentinel system contains supporting information regarding purely domestic TERRORISTS.

1.8 Pursuant to Paragraph (2) of HSPD-6, the NCTC is mandated to "provide [TSC] with access to all appropriate information or intelligence in the [NCTC's] custody, possession, or control that [TSC] requires to perform its functions." NCTC fulfills this function by providing TSC's TSDB with U//FOUO information about KNOWN or SUSPECTED TERRORISTS from NCTC's TIDE and by providing access to TIDE Online, a read-only copy of the TIDE database, to those in the watchlisting community who require access.

1.9 NCTC's establishment by the President was codified by section 1021 of the Intelligence Reform and Terrorism Prevention Act of 2004 (IRTPA).[8] Pursuant to IRTPA, NCTC shall "serve as the central and shared knowledge bank on KNOWN and SUSPECTED TERRORISTS and international terror groups." In addition, NCTC "may, consistent with applicable law, the direction of the President, and guidelines referred to in [the statute], receive intelligence pertaining exclusively to domestic counterterrorism from any Federal, State, or local government or other source necessary to fulfill its responsibilities and retain and disseminate such intelligence."[9]

1.9.1 All Departments and Agencies arc required to provide NCTC with all TERRORISM INFORMATION . Due to the amount of information involved, only a subset of this information is provided in the NCTC prescribed format designed to facilitate direct ingestion into the TIDE. NOMINATING DEPARTMENTS and AGENCIES , however, should remain focused on reviewing and watchlisting TERRORISM INFORMATION from datasets most likely to contain information about KNOWN or SUSPECTED TERRORISTS.

1.10 On August 27, 2004, the President issued Homeland Security Presidential Directive 11 (HSPD-11), which "builds upon HSPD-6," to enhance TERRORLST-related screening to more effectively detect and interdict SUSPECTED TERRORISTS and TERRORIST ACTIVITIES. HSPD-11 defines "SUSPECTED TERRORISTS" as "individuals known or reasonably suspected to be or have been engaged in conduct constituting, in preparation for, in aid of, or related to TERRORISM and TERRORIST ACTIVITIES."

1.11 To enhance information sharing, another key component of the consolidated terrorist watchlisting system, the President issued Executive Order 13388, which provides that the head of each Agency that possesses or acquires TERRORISM INFORMATION shall promptly give access to that information to the head of cach other Agency that has counterterrorism functions. [10]

1.12 On June 5, 2008, the President issued Homeland Security Presidential Directive 24 (HSPD-24) to further build upon the TERRORIST screening policies announced in HSPD-6 and HSPD-11 to protect the nation from TERRORISTS by enhancing the use of biometrics. In HSPD-24, the President directed that ". . . agencies, shall, to the fullest extent permitted by law, make available to other agencies all biomctric and associated biographic and contextual information associated with persons for whom there is an articulable and reasonable basis for suspicion that they pose a threat to national security (emphasis added). HSPD-24 underscores the value of biometrics in achieving effective TERRORISM screening and emphasizes the need for a layered approach to identification and screening of individuals, as no single mechanism is sufficient.

1.13 The relevant TERRORISM screening Presidential Directives use words and phrases to describe a KNOWN or SUSPECTED TERRORIST subject to TERRORIST screening without defining them: "TERRORIST INFORMATION" (HSPD-6), "TERRORISM" (HSPD-6), "appropriately suspected" (HSPD-6), "reasonably suspected" (HSPD-11), and "articulable and reasonable basis for suspicion" (HSPD-24). Thus, previous watchlisting guidance supplied definitions of key terms and the standard that would apply to terrorist watchlisting decisions.

1.14 Neither HSPD-6 nor HSPD-11 defines "TERRORISM and/or TERRORIST ACTIVITIES." While federal law contains numerous definitions of "terrorism"[11] , for watchlisting purposes under this Guidance, "TERRORISM and/or TERRORIST ACTIVITIES" combine elements from various federal definitions and are considered to:

1.14.1 involve violent acts or acts dangerous to human life, property, or infrastructure which may be a violation of U.S. law, or may have been, if those acts were committed in the United States; and,

1.14.2 appear to be intended—
1.14.2.1 to intimidate or coerce a civilian population;
1.14.2.2 to influence the policy of a government by intimidation or coercion; or,
1.14.2.3 to affect the conduct of a government by mass destruction, assassination,

kidnapping, or hostage-taking.

1.15 This includes activities that facilitate or support TERRORISM and/or TERRORIST ACTIVITIES such as providing a safe house, transportation, communications, funds, transfer of funds or other material benefit, false documentation or identification, weapons (including chemical, biological, or radiological weapons), explosives, or training for the commission of an act of TERRORISM and/or TERRORIST ACTIVITY.

1.16 HSPD-24 speaks in terms of "articulable and reasonable basis for suspicion" to describe a KNOWN or SUSPECTED TERRORIST who should be watchlistcd and represents the President's most recent explanation concerning U.S. policy regarding the individuals who pose a threat to national security and should be screened to better protect the American people. Accordingly, that standard has been adopted and is clarified in this Watchlisting Guidance in Chapter 3, Section II.

1.17 On December 16, 2005, in accordance with section 1016 of IRTPA, the President issued a Memorandum for the Heads of Executive Departments and Agencies prescribing the guidelines and requirements in support of the creation and implementation of the Information Sharing Environment (ISE). In Guideline 5 of that Memorandum, the President directed, as he had earlier in Executive Order 13353[12] , that the information privacy rights and other legal rights of Americans must be protected and that guidelines be developed and approved to ensure that "such rights are protected in the development and use of the ISE." In December 2006, the President approved for issuance the ISE Privacy Guidelines by the Program Manager.[13]

1.18 A second addendum to the TSC MOU, Addendum B[14], which supplements and incorporates by reference all provisions of the TSC MOU, superseded Addendum A and became effective on January 18, 2007. The Directors of National Intelligence, NCTC, and the TSC joined as signatories in Addendum B. Paragraph 7 of Addendum B introduces the term TERRORIST IDENTIFIERS to more clearly describe the type of TERRORIST identity elements that are deemed U//FOUO, without regard to the classification of the source material from which it is drawn. TERRORIST IDENTIFIERS include those listed in Addendum B (i.e., names and aliases; dates of birth; places of birth; unique identifying numbers; passport information; countries of origin and nationality; physical identifiers; known locations; photographs or renderings; fingerprints or other biometric data; employment data; license plate numbers; and any other TERRORIST IDENTIFIERS that ORIGINATORS specifically provide for passage to the TSC). For example, email addresses and phone numbers are increasingly useful for screening purposes. ORIGINATORS should mark email addresses and phone numbers as U//FOUO whenever possible and pass these TERRORIST IDENTIFIERS to NCTC to forward to the TSC for inclusion in TSDB. ORIGINATORS are encouraged to provide all relevant and unclassified information, to include social media information when appropriate.

III. CONSTITUTIONALLY PROTECTED ACTIVITIES

1.19 **First Amendment.** First Amendment protected activity alone shall not be the basis for nominating an individual for inclusion on the Terrorist Watchlist.[15] The following arc examples of protected Constitutional activities:

> 1.19.1 **Free Speech.** The exercise of free speech, guaranteed by the U.S. Constitution, includes more than simply speaking on a controversial topic in the town square. It includes such

symbolic or other written, oral and expressive activities as carrying placards in a parade, sending letters to a newspaper editor, wearing a tee shirt with a political message, placing a bumper sticker critical of the President on one's car, and publishing books or articles. The common thread in these examples is conveying a public message or an idea through words or deeds. Speech that may be repugnant to ideas of the majority may still be protected by the U.S. Constitution. For the purpose of this Watchlisting Guidance, the right of protected free speech under the U.S. Constitution applies to U.S. PERSONS wherever they are located and to non-U.S. PERSONS located inside the United States. The right of protected free speech, however, is not unlimited and may not extend to some lawless action.

1.19.2 **Exercise of Religion.** The free exercise of religion covers any form of worship of a deity - even forms that are not widely known or practiced - as well as the right not to worship any deity. Protected religious exercise also extends to dress that is worn or food that is eaten for a religious purpose, attendance at a facility used for religious practice, observance of the Sabbath, raising money for evangelical or missionary purposes, and proselytizing.

1.19.3 **Freedom of the Press.** Freedom of the press includes such matters as reasonable access to news-making events, the making of documentaries, and the posting of "blogs."

1.19.4 **Freedom of Peaceful Assembly.** Freedom of peaceful assembly, often called the right to freedom of association, includes gathering with others to protest government action, or to rally or demonstrate in favor of, or in opposition to, a social cause. The right to peaceful assembly includes more than just public demonstrations - it includes, as well, the posting of group websites on the Internet, recruiting others to a lawful cause, marketing a message, and fundraising, which all are protected First Amendment activities if they are conducted in support of an organizational, political, religious, or social cause.

1.19.5 **Petition the Government for Redress of Grievances.** The right to petition the government for redress of grievances includes, for example, writing letters to Congress, carrying a placard outside the city hall that delivers a political message, recruiting others to one's cause, and lobbying Congress or an Executive Agency for a particular result.

1.20 **Equal Protection.** The Equal Protection Clause of the U.S. Constitution provides in part that: "No State shall make or enforce any law which shall ... deny to any person within its jurisdiction the equal protection of the laws." The U.S. Supreme Court has made it clear that this applies as well to the official acts of U.S. Government personnel. Nominations, therefore, shall not be based solely on race, ethnicity, national origin, or religious affiliation. Any activities relating to this Guidance that are based solely on such considerations are invidious by definition, and therefore, unconstitutional.

IV. WATCHLISTING POLICIES

1.21 **Watchlisting Disclosures.** The general policy of the U.S. Government is to neither confirm nor deny an individual's watchlist status. In addition to the provisions in Addendum B to the TSC MOU, which require NOMINATOR approval before TSDB information can be used in any process that might result in public disclosure, the 2007 Memorandum of Understanding on Terrorist Watchlist Redress Procedures (Redress MOU)[16] requires SCREENERS to contact the TSC if it receives a request for information or records that might reveal an individual's watchlist status. Approval would also be required from any entity which provided information used by a NOMINATOR during a nomination. Per the Redress MOU, ORIGINATING and NOMINATING AGENCIES are obligated to support SCREENER determinations - both at the administrative level and in litigation - and provide appropriate information, including unclassified substitutes as necessary. TSC, in conjunction with NCTC, the NOMINATORS, and the Department of Justice (DOJ), as appropriate, will ensure that representations regarding an individual's potential watchlist status are properly coordinated and approved.

1.22 **Legal or Use Restrictions.** Because information in the TSDB comes overwhelmingly from intelligence sources and methods or sensitive law enforcement techniques, Paragraph 12 of Addendum B to the TSC MOU[17] requires that any recipient of information from the TSDB seeking to use TERRORIST identity information in any legal or administrative process or proceeding obtain NOMINATOR approval before doing so. Approval from the entity which provided the information, if other than the NOMINATOR, is also required. Additionally, information from Foreign Intelligence Surveillance Act (F1SA) collections may only be used in a proceeding with the advance authorization of the Attorney General. Therefore, any SCREENER seeking to use TSDB information in any process or proceeding must contact TSC so that TSC can assist in obtaining approval from the NOMINATOR, owner of the information, or Attorney General, as required.

1.23 In addition to the foregoing restrictions, there are restrictions on sharing information with foreign governments. Any TERRORIST IDENTIFIER (as described in Addendum B to the TSC MOU) will be deemed U//FOUO and shared with the watchlisting community and foreign governments for watchlisting purposes pursuant to the terms of the TSC MOU. Accordingly, NOMINA TORS should include, as appropriate, TERRORIST IDENTIFIERS in documents that contain non-releasable warnings (e.g., a report is not releasable to xxx/yyy/zzz countries), unless the TERRORIST IDENTIFIERS are restricted by some other authority that limits dissemination. If U.S. PERSON information is otherwise authorized for release to the foreign government, the non-releasable warning is disabled to allow dissemination of the information.

V. WATCHLISTING STANDARD: IDENTIFYING AND SUBSTANTIVE DEROGATORY CRITERIA

1.24 Before a KNOWN or SUSPECTED TERRORIST is added to the Terrorist Watchlist, TSC reviews the nomination to determine whether it meets the following minimum identifying criteria and minimum substantive derogatory criteria for inclusion in the TSDB.

> 1.24.1 **Minimum Identifying Criteria.** Each nomination must contain minimum identifying criteria for inclusion into the TSDB. Without this minimum identifying data, the nomination is not eligible for inclusion into the TSDB, or any of the TSC's supported systems. Chapter 2 sets forth guidance regarding both the minimum identifying biometric and biographic criteria for inclusion into the TSDB. Although TIDE accepts records containing less than these minimum criteria, such records will not be exported either to the TSDB for watchlisting or to the various supported systems used by the SCREENERS absent an exception described in the Watchlisting Guidance.

> 1.24.2 **Minimum Substantive Derogatory Criteria.** In addition to the minimum identifying criteria, nominations to the TSDB are accepted based on a REASONABLE SUSPICION that the individual is a KNOWN or SUSPECTED TERRORIST derived from the totality of the

information reviewed for nomination.[18] To demonstrate that the nomination has sufficient indicia of reliability to support this REASONABLE SUSPICION determination, NOMINATING AGENCIES should implement processes designed to ensure that nominations are free from errors, that recalled or revised information is reviewed regularly, and that necessary corrections to nominations based on those revisions/retractions are made. NOMINATING AGENCIES should, to the extent possible given the nature of the reporting, verify the accuracy and reliability of the information included in nominations, in some cases, the NOMINATING AGENCY may not be able to evaluate the reliability of the information received; however, in such situations, the NOMINATING AGENCY can ensure that the information provided is an accurate representation of the information obtained. Chapter 3 sets forth further guidance regarding the application of the REASONABLE SUSPICION standard to TSDB nominations.

VI. WATCHLISTING PROCESS OVERVIEW

1.25 The authorities referenced in Section II of this Chapter created the framework for the watchlisting enterprise by combining various functions of existing government entities and joining them to new organizations with counterterrorism responsibilities. The resulting watchlisting enterprise consists of ORIGINATORS, NOMINATORS, AGGREGATORS, SCREENERS and encountering agencies that are supported by the community-wide collection, nomination, and consolidation processes.

1.26 **ORIGINATORS, NOMINATORS, AGGREGATORS, and SCREENERS.** All Executive Departments and Agencies have responsibility for collecting, collating, and sharing TERRORISM INFORMATION to support the watchlisting process. They are called ORIGINATORS because they initially collect and identify information supporting the conclusion that an individual is a KNOWN or SUSPECTED TERRORIST. An ORIGINATOR is the Department or Agency that has appropriate subject matter interest and classification authority and collects TERRORISM INFORMATION (*i.e.,* raw information) and disseminates it or TERRORIST IDENTIFIERS to other U.S. Government entities via an intelligence report (i.e., finished intelligence) or other mechanism. In general, when an ORIGINATOR has identified international TERRORISM INFORMATION and determines that information should be provided to NCTC, the ORIGINATOR takes on the NOMINATOR role. A NOMINATOR is a Federal Department or Agency that has information to indicate that an individual meets the criteria for a KNOWN or SUSPECTED TERRORIST and nominates that individual to TIDE and the TSDB based on information that originated with that Agency.

1.27 While all NOMINATORS have the duty of upholding informational standards, the NCTC and TSC are distinctly responsible for ensuring data quality and the integrity of their respective repositories. NCTC and TSC are themselves potential N O M I N A T O R S . Analysts from the NCTC may discover an individual who is eligible for watchlisting while reviewing all-source information. In these cases, NCTC analysts will request that the ORIGINATOR submit a nomination for inclusion into TIDE; or, on a limited basis or during exigent circumstances, NCTC analysts may update TIDE directly with a disseminated report and noticc to the ORIGINATOR(S). In instances where disseminated reporting is used to enhance TIDE, NCTC will provide notice back to the collecting agency via TIDE. TSC may also nominate TERRORISM INFORMATION received pursuant to TERRORISM screening conducted by foreign governments.

1.28 NCTC and TSC are responsible for reviewing both newly nominated individuals, as well as subsets of existing records, to determine if additional and/or enhancement (research) is required to locate missing information critical to the watchlisting process. In some cases, this will require research to locate additional DEROGATORY INFORMATION to meet the minimum substantive derogatory criteria for watchlisting. In other cases, this will require research to locate additional biographic or biometric identifiers, in order to provide a comprehensive record maximizing the probability of confirming a POSITIVE MATCH to an identity contained in the TSDB.

1.29 AGGREGATORS are those who receive and hold TERRORISM INFORMATION and certain other non-TERRORLSM INFORMATION they are authorized to receive and retain. For example, two of NCTC's main statutory missions are to serve as the (1) central and shared knowledge bank on KNOWN or SUSPECTED TERRORISTS and (2) primary organization in the U.S. Government for analyzing and integrating all intelligence information possessed or acquired by the U.S. Government pertaining to TERRORISM and counterterrorism.[19]

1.30 TSC takes on the role of an AGGREGATOR when a KNOWN or SUSPECTED TERRORIST is encountered and the individual's record is enhanced or updated with ENCOUNTER-related information. As noted in Paragraphs 1.1 and 1.7, the TSC manages the watchlisting process and plays a key role in helping Departments and Agencies determine whether an ENCOUNTER with a member of the public is one with a KNOWN or SUSPECTED TERRORIST. Additional TERRORISM INFORMATION or TERRORIST IDENTIFIERS are generated during ENCOUNTERS and the Encounter Management Application (EMA)[20] uses that information to update records of KNOWN o r SUSPECTED TERRORISTS.

1.31 SCREENERS vet against the TSDB to determine if an individual is a possible match to a KNOWN or SUSPECTED TERRORIST in the TSDB. SCREENERS can include federal, state, local, tribal, territorial, or foreign governments and certain private entities. Screening officials include homeland security officers, consular affairs officers, transportation safety personnel, and officials of foreign governments with whom the United States has entered into a TERRORISM SCREENING INFORMATION sharing agreement pursuant to HSPD-6. Certain Departments and Agencies have components which perform both screening and law enforcement duties. If a SCREENER believes an individual may be on the Watchlist, the screener contacts the TSC's Terrorist Screening Operations Center (TSOC). The TSOC will determine whether the individual the SCREENER has encountered is, in fact, a POSITIVE MATCH to the individual who is on the Terrorist Watchlist. The TSOC may also notify the FBI's Counterterrorism Division (CTD) that there has been a positive ENCOUNTER with a watchlistcd subject. TSC's Terrorist Screening Operations Unit (TSOU) coordinates the appropriate operational response to the ENCOUNTER. Based on the TERRORISM INFORMATION made available by the ORIGINATING AGENCY , the SCREENER will take action based upon its specific authorities (e.g., requiring additional screening at an airport checkpoint, denying a visa application, determining admissibility into the United States) and follow appropriate ENCOUNTER procedures, as set forth in Chapter 5.

1.32 **Collection, Nomination, Consolidation and the Use of the Terrorist Watchlist to Perform Screening Processes.** The following is a chart depicting the collection, TERRORIST nomination, consolidation and screening processes:

1.32 Collection, Nomination, Consolidation and the Use of the Terrorist Watchlist to Perform Screening Processes. The following is a chart depicting the collection, TERRORIST nomination, consolidation and screening processes:

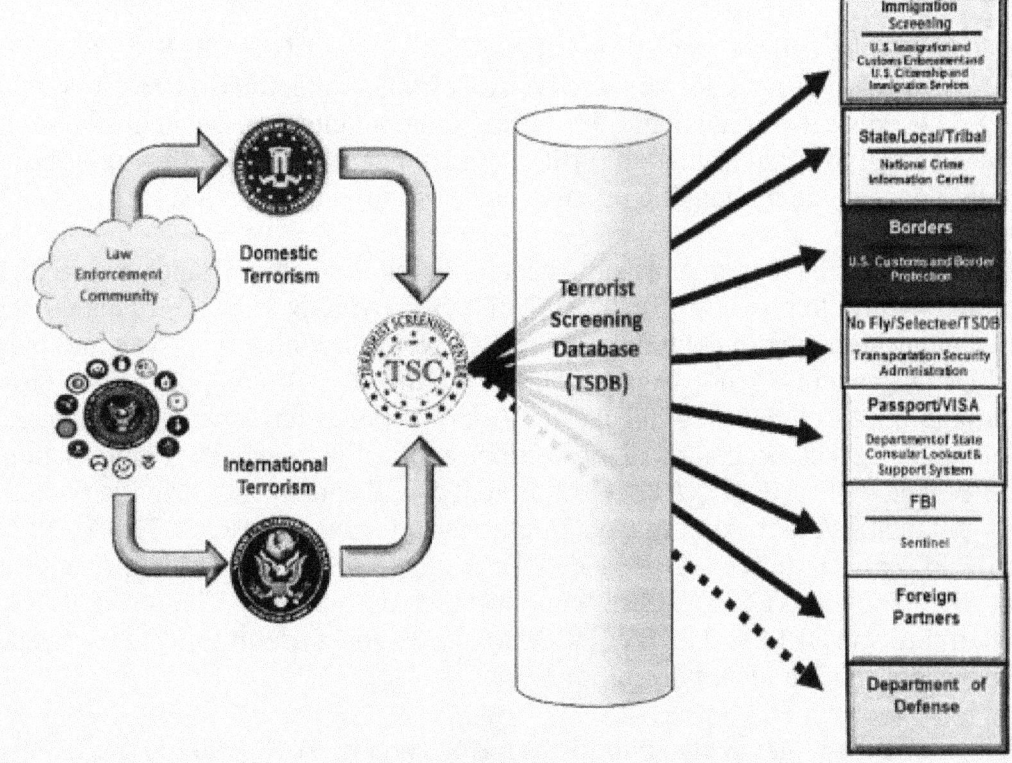

1.33 The arrows fade inside the TSDB cylinder because not every nomination from NCTC (for international TERRORISM) or the FBI (for domestic TERRORISM) is exported from the TSDB to SCREENERS (represented by the multi-colored blocks at the far right of the chart).[21] For example, certain categories of individuals that do not meet the minimum identifying criteria (see Chapter 2, Section II) or the REASONABLE SUSPICION standard (see Chapter 3, Section II) can be watchlisted to support immigration and visa screening activities by DHS and DOS (see Chapter 3, Section V) but are not exported to state/local/tribal SCREENERS or foreign partners. Similarly, when ORIGINATORS provide FRAGMENTARY INFORMATION to NCTC for inclusion in TIDE, such information will not be exported from TIDE to the TSDB, unless the NOMINATING AGENCY believes there is REASONABLE SUSPICION to believe that the individual is a KNOWN or SUSPECTED TERRORIST. FRAGMENTARY INFORMATION is provided to NCTC where it can be further analyzed, connected to existing information, and added to TIDE for export to TSDB because NCTC, and not individual ORIGINATORS, has access to all the information available to the U.S. Government on a KNOWN or SUSPECTED TERRORIST.

VII. ROLES AND RESPONSIBILITES FOR THE WATCHLISTING AND SCREENING COMMUNITY

1.34 Delineation of roles and responsibilities of NOMINATING AGENCIES, SCREENERS, NC TC, and the TSC is critical to provide for an effective and efficient integrated Terrorist Watchlist enterprise. While IISPD-6 describes the broad mandate of developing an integrated watchlist system, and the TSC MOU provides a level of detail needed to fulfill that mandate, further clarification is required to ensure there are neither gaps in the nomination process, nor wasteful redundancies.

1.35 Pursuant to USPD-6, Departments and Agencies in the Executive Branch are required, to the extent permitted by law, to provide TERRORIST INFORMATION to NCTC. This process will be accomplished either through direct nomination to NCTC, or through a specific component designated by a Federal Department or Agency head for doing so (e.g., all DOJ components are directed to nominate through the FBI; DHS Intelligence and Analysis (l&A) has oversight responsibility for all DHS nominations). Except as detailed in the sections applicable to expedited nominations (see Paragraphs 1.58 and 1.59), NOMINATING AGENCIES will endeavor to provide comprehensive nominations and include the maximum amount of identifying and DEROGATORY INFORMATION.[22] NOMINATING DEPARTMENTS AND AGENCIES should prioritize the identification of new KNOWN or SUSPECTED TERRORISTS who meet the REASONABLE SUSPICION standard, along with the identifying and DEROGATORY INFORMATION most useful to watchlisting, and screening effort, as well as assisting in identity resolution.

1.36 Each Department or Agency that nominates a KNOWN or SUSPECTED TERRORIST to NCTC for watchlisting is under a continuing obligation to provide NCTC with newly identified DEROGATORY INFORMATION or exculpatory information obtained by that Department or Agency. Each Department or Agency also has the responsibility to provide NCTC with newly identified identifying and DEROGATORY INFORMATION obtained from their Department or Agency, regardless if they were the original NOMINATING AGENCY.

1.37 With the noted exception of the Visa Viper Program, Departments and Agencies should not nominate KNOWN or SUSPECTED TERRORISTS to NCTC based on information that they do not originate without first coordinating with the ORIGINATOR.

VIII. QUALITY CONTROL MEASURES

1.38 In order to produce and maintain the most reliable and accurate information in TIDE, TSDB, and screening databases, quality control is considered a responsibility of all entities. NOMINATING DEPARTMENTS AND AGENCIES must establish and maintain processes, including appropriate training and guidance, to ensure information transmitted to NCTC is consistent with the source of the information.

1.39 **HSPD-6 Requirements.** HSPD-6 requires the TSC to maintain thorough, accurate, and current information concerning KNOWN or SUSPECTED TERRORISTS. For watchlisting purposes, "current" means information that the NOMINATING AGENCY reasonably believes is valid and accurate. The requirement that information be current does not necessarily preclude information that is several years old from being included in the TSDB if there is no reason to believe the information may have changed (e.g., information regarding an individual's date of birth or TERRORIST ACTIVITY was collected 20 years ago but has not been superseded by additional information is still relevant). NOMINATORS should consider the date of the DEROGATORY INFORMATION in the context of analyzing the overall quality of the data, as well as the severity of the threat, to determine whether the individual warrants watchlisting. The date of the DEROGATORY INFORMATION may refer to both the date the information is collected (such as a report that was collected 50 years ago) as well as the date of the information that is referenced in the reporting (such as a recent report that references an event that occurred 50 years ago).

1.40 TSC MOU Obligations. Paragraph 15 of the TSC MOU provides that the TSC "will determine, according to criteria established jointly with the entity responsible for each supported system, which supported screening processes will query that entry in the consolidated TERRORIST screening database." Pursuant to that paragraph, the TSC is required to "make these determinations based on criteria and procedures developed in coordination with the Parties to this Memorandum and in consultation with the heads of appropriate Federal Departments and Agencies based on factors, including but not limited to, the following:

> 1.40.1 the nature of the person's association with TERRORISM;
>
> 1.40.2 the quality of the data, including credibility, reliability, and extent of corroboration; and,
>
> 1.40.3 the extent of uniquely identifying data.. . . "[23]

1.41 Provide Guidance and Training. Each Agency will provide guidance on the watchlisting business process. Analysts will receive periodic refresher training, as needed.

1.42 NOMINATING AGENCY Procedures. Each NOMINATOR providing international TERRORIST watchlisting nominations to NCTC is responsible for the accuracy of its information and has a continuing responsibility to notify NCTC of any changes that affect the validity or reliability of such information.[24] NCTC analysts will review each nomination for TERRORIST watchlisting prior to its inclusion into TIDE and its export to the TSDB.

1.43 Each NOMINATING AGENCY should implement processes designed to ensure that nominations are free from errors, that recalled or revised information is reviewed regularly, and that necessary corrections to nominations based on those revisions/retractions are made. NOMINATING AGENCIES should, to the extent possible given the nature of the reporting, verify the accuracy and reliability of the information included in nominations. The following represents the type of processes that each NOMINATING AGENCY shall develop that are tailored to each Agency's particular mission and operational environment:

> 1.43.1 **Develop Adequate Factual Predicate.** Each NOMINATING AGENCY will seek to obtain as much DEROGATORY INFORMATION and identifying information as practicable concerning the KNOWN or SUSPECTED TERRORIST who is being nominated.
>
> 1.43.2 **Provide Guidance and Training.** Each NOMINATING AGENCY will provide guidance on the TERRORIST watchlisting nomination process and ensure that analysts involved in the nomination process arc trained on a periodic basis.
>
> 1.43.3 **Require Quality Assurance Review.** Each NOMINATING AGENCY will use a quality

assurance process to review nominations for accuracy prior to forwarding the information to NCTC.

1.43.4 **Heightened Review for U.S. PERSONS.** The nominations of U.S. PERSONS require special considerations and procedures.[25] See Paragraph 3.15.

1.43.5 **U.S. PERSON Determinations.** NOMINATORS must take reasonable steps to determine whether an individual is a U.S. PERSON.

1.43.6 **U.S. PERSON Review and Confirmation.** Nominations of U.S. PERSONS to the Terrorist Watchlist shall be reviewed by the NOMINATING AGENCY'S legal counsel or a designated reviewer to confirm that the REASONABLE SUSPICION standard has been met or that the nomination meets an exception to the REASONABLE SUSPICION standard, and to ensure that the nomination conforms to Agency specific U.S. PERSON authorities and guidelines.

1.43.7 **Reliability and Accuracy Limitations.** Nominations will includc any limitations on the reliability or accuracy of the information.

1.43.8 **Periodic Reviews.** The NOMINATING AGENCY will conduct periodic reviews of their nominations of U.S. PERSONS to the Terrorist Watchlist, at minimum on an annual basis, when there is no corresponding FBI investigation to ensure that the U.S. PERSON continues to meet watchlisting criteria.

1.43.9 **Redress Procedures.** As per the establishment of a formal watchlist redress process (see Chapter 1, Section XI), entities involved in the watchlisting proccss shall establish internal reviews and redress procedures.

1.44 Each NOMINATING AGENCY will have procedures that facilitate the prevention, identification, and correction of any errors in information that is shared as part of the watchlisting process. Procedures will include the review of retractions and/or corrections of information that may have been used to support a nomination. In cases where a retraction or other information has become available, the NOMINATING AGENCY will promptly send a watchlist removal request or modification, as appropriate, to NCTC. Each NOMINATING AGENCY must provide notice of any errors or outdated information to NCTC immediately unless there is an articulated reason why such notification could not be made immediately. NCTC will process and transmit to TSC such corrections upon receipt.

1.45 **NCTC Review.** In addition to review by NCTC analysts, NCTC will employ a quality control proccss to ensure that all standards and appropriate procedures have been employed, the data is accurate, and the presentation of the material is clear, concise, and complies with established definitions and conventions. NCTC must also have processes and procedures in place to ensure the information documented in TIDE and provided to the TSC is accurately transcribed. NCTC shall ensure there is a process in place for review and/or auditing of TIDE records.

1.46 **TSC Review.** TSC personnel will review the nominations received as described in Paragraph 1.56. TSC personnel evaluate whether nominations meet watchlisting standards and weigh, as appropriate, all-source analysis before accepting or rejecting a nomination. The TSC has a critical role to play in quality control, as the TSC review is the last step before any record (including a biometric nomination where no name is available) is sent to various screening systems. As with NCTC, the TSC should ensure there is a process in placc for review and/or auditing of TSC nominations and TSC records.

IX. NOMINATION PROCEDURES

1.47 **Distinctions between U.S. PERSONS under Executive Order 12333 and Aliens under the Immigration and Nationality Act.** This Watchlisting Guidance generally adopts the definition of U.S. PERSON from Executive Order 12333 (as amended) for nomination procedures. Executive Order 12333 defines a U.S. PERSON as "A United States citizen, an alien known by the intelligence element concerned to be a permanent resident alien, an unincorporated association substantially composed of United States citizens or permanent resident aliens, or a corporation incorporated in the United States, except for a corporation directed or controlled by a foreign government or governments." The Watchlisting Guidance also contains certain exceptions to the minimum substantive derogatory standards for TERRORIST watchlisting that support immigration and visa screening activities by the DHS and DOS to determine whether ineligibilities exist for admission to the United States or visa adjudication pursuant to the Immigration and Nationality Act (INA). Because the INA defines "aliens" as any person not a citizen or national of the United States, the INA admissibility provisions also apply to Lawful Permanent Residents (LPRs), in certain circumstances, who are considered U.S. PERSONS under Executive Order 12333. Consequently, NCTC developed a mechanism in TIDE to identify and distinguish U.S. citizens from non-U.S. citizens in order to further distinguish between "aliens" under the INA and U.S. PERSONS under Executive Order 12333.[26]

1.48 **ORIGINATOR'S Nominations Procedures.** As mentioned in Paragraph 1.26, when an ORIGINATOR becomes a NOMINATOR, it prepares a nomination document and forwards it to NCTC through the NOMINATOR tool.

> 1.48.1 As a general rule, NCTC will attach all disseminated communications (cablcs or forms) to the TERRORIST identities rccord as a "source" document, which will be available on NCTC Current or the Joint Worldwide Intelligence Communications System (JWICS) to individuals who have been granted access to TIDE.

> 1.48.2 Because NCTC is the conduit for passing international TERRORISM INFORMATION to TSC for TERRORISM screening purposes, there is no longer a need to send watchlist requests to multiple Government Agencies. By sending a Terrorist Watchlist nomination cable to NCTC, all potential U.S. Government TERRORISM screening responsibilities should be accounted for.

> 1.48.3 The DOJ has approved a Protocol to govern TERRORIST nominations for its non-FBI components, which requires components to provide the FBI with all TERRORISM INFORMATION.[27] The FBI is responsible for submitting watchlisting nominations based on information received from other DOJ components pursuant to the FBI's nomination procedures.

> 1.48.4 DHS has designated the Under Secretary for I&A as the Executive Agent for DHS' centralized TERRORIST watchlisting process and he/she shall be responsible for providing a DHS wide-mechanism for nominating all identifying or DEROGATORY INFORMATION about KNOWN or SUSPECTED TERRORISTS to TIDE. DHS I&A is also responsible for providing training/certification programs to the components.

1.49 In providing information to NCTC for inclusion into TIDE, the ORIGINATOR is responsible for determining whether it may, by law, provide the information to NCTC, in accordancc with section 1021(d)(6) of IRTPA. This information shall be provided with any applicable caveats or dissemination controls, which will be reflected in TIDE. The biographic and biometric identifiers derived from this information will be deemed U//FOUO for passage to TSDB unless the ORIGINATOR designates them as "TIDE Restricted," as outlined in Addendum B to the TSC MOU.

1.50 **NCTC Actions and Processes.** NCTC reviews TERRORIST nominations from Federal Departments or Agencies (NOMINATORS) as described in Paragraph 1.28.

1.51 In determining whether an individual is a KNOWN or SUSPECTED TERRORIST, NCTC will rely on the designation of "KNOWN TERRORIST" provided by the NOMINATOR as presumptively valid. This presumption can be overcome if NCTC has specific and credible information within its possession that such designation is not appropriate, at which point NCTC will provide such information to the NOMINATOR.

1.52 In reviewing whether to include the TERRORISM INFORMATION about the KNOWN or SUSPECTED TERRORIST in TIDE, NCTC reviews the totality of information. The totality of information is evaluated based on the experience of the reviewer, and the facts and rational inferences that may be drawn from those facts, including past conduct, current actions, and credible intelligence conccrning future conduct. As part of this review, NCTC will determine if the information pertains to, or is related to, TERRORISM. TIDE includes TERRORISM INFORMATION on KNOWN or SUSPECTED TERRORISTS and may include additional TERRORISM INFORMATION beyond what meets the minimum substantive derogatory and identifying criteria required for nominations to the TSDB, as described in Paragraph 1.24. Upon conclusion of NCTC's review, NCTC will either accept or reject the nomination:

> 1.52.1 **Accept Nomination.** If a nomination contains TERRORISM INFORMATION, NCTC will create or enhance the associated TIDE record with the data contained in the nomination. If the minimum substantive derogatory and identifying criteria are met, NCTC will forward the TERRORIST IDENTIFIERS to the TSC for placement in TSDB with the NOMINATOR'S watchlist recommendation.

> 1.52.2 **Reject Nomination.** If a nomination does not contain TERRORISM INFORMATION, NCTC may reject the nomination. NCTC will review rejected nominations and search holdings for additional data that may support a TERRORISM INFORMATION finding. If no information is found to support the nomination, NCTC will notify the NOMINATING AGENCY of the rejection.

1.53 **Types of records in TIDE.** There are two types of records in TIDE:

> 1.53.1 **TERRORIST Records.** The vast majority of records in TIDE are for KNOWN or SUSPECTED international TERRORISTS. These records are labeled "TERRORISTS." Only a small percentage of TERRORIST records in TIDE concern U.S. PERSONS.

> 1.53.2 **Non-TERRORIST Records.** A small percentage of records in TIDE are identified and labeled "Non-TERRORISTS."[28] These records are generally of familial family members or associates of KNOWN or SUSPECTED TERRORISTS and assist DOS and DHS in, for example, adjudicating visas and immigration processing, or assist the IC in tracking KNOWN

TERRORISTS. These "Non-TERRORISTS" include:

1.53.2.1 **Alien Spouses and Children of TERRORISTS.** Based on section 212(a)(3)(B)(i)(IX) of the INA, alien spouses and children of TERRORISTS may be inadmissible to the United States.[29] TIDE exports records pertaining to alien spouses and children of alien international TERRORISTS (also known as TIDE Category Code 17) to support immigration and visa screening activities by DOS and DHS;

1.53.2.2 **Other Relatives.** TIDE also includes "non- TERRORIST" records of individuals who have a close relationship to a KNOWN or SUSPECTED international TERRORIST but are not alien spouses or children of a TERRORIST. For instance, the father or brother of a TERRORIST could have a record in TIDE (also known as TIDE Category Code 160). Thus, these "other relatives" could be U.S. PERSONS or non-U.S. PERSONS. Identifiers for these other relations reside in TIDE but are not exported to the TSC for watchlisting, absent independent DEROGATORY INFORMATION. Instead, these records may be retained in TIDE for analytic purposes;

1.53.2.3 **Passports.** Unrecovered lost or stolen passports in the hands of international TERRORISTS (also known as TIDE Category Code 89);

1.53.2.4 **Associates.** Individuals who have a defined relationship with the KNOWN or SUSPECTED TERRORIST, but whose involvement with the KNOWN or SUSPECTED TERRORIST'S activities is unknown (also known as TIDE Category Code 50);

1.53.2.5 **Individuals with a Possible Nexus to TERRORISM.** Individuals with a possible nexus to TERRORISM and/or TERRORIST ACTIVITY but for whom additional DEROGATORY INFORMATION is needed to meet the REASONABLE SUSPICION standard (also known as TIDE Category Code 99).

1.54 **Identification of U.S. PERSON Status in TIDE.** NCTC analysts will review the totality of information available on a subject to discern U . S . PERSON status prior to creating or enhancing a record in TIDE, whenever possible. For existing TIDE records, this status is available to the analyst in the first field of the TIDE record. In case of external nominations or ENHANCEMENTS from the IC, the standard nomination template provides a means for NOMINATORS to identify U.S. PERSON status pursuant to Executive Order 12333 and the Agency's specific guidelines. The U.S. PERSON status field on the standard nomination template is a required field and it is the responsibility of each NOMINATING AGENCY to ensure the field is properly annotated in accordance with established policy.

1.55 **Types of Records in TIDE and the TSDB.** Not all records in TIDE are included in the TSDB. For example, records with FRAGMENTARY INFORMATION that do not meet the minimum derogatory standard or records that do not meet identifying information criteria remain in TIDE and are not included in the TSDB, absent direction for temporary, threat based categories pursuant to Paragraph 1.59.[30] The nominations process for TIDE records that will be considered for entry in the TSDB begins with an automated data transfer process that moves an individual TIDE record containing the identity of a KNOWN or SUSPECTED TERRORIST or other exportable category or record nominated for watchlisting to the TSDB.

1.56 **TSC Actions and Processes.** The TSC's Single Review Queue (SR.Q) enables the TSC's

Nominations and Data Integrity Unit (NDIU) to review each KNOWN or SUSPECTED TERRORIST record nomination to ensure it meets the watchlisting standard.[31] The SRQ also helps ensure that all qualified records are made available to the appropriate SCREENERS for use in TERRORISM screening. During the SRO process, every request to add, modify, or delete a TSDB record is reviewed by a TSC analyst to ensure the accuracy of watchlisting records and the removal of inaccurate records from TSDB.

1.56.1 Within the TSC's NDIU, experienced analysts and/or designated Agency representatives serve as Subject Matter Experts (SMEs) with respect to specific databases (e.g., No Fly or Selectee List) that receive TSDB data for TERRORISM screening purposes. The NDIU currently has four types of SMEs who specialize in the information/systems from their respective organizations: DHS/Transportation Security Administration (TSA) for the No Fly, Selectee and Expanded Selectee Lists, FBI for National Crime Information Center (NCIC)/KNOWN or SUSPECTED TERRORIST File (KSTF), DOS for the Consular Consolidated Database (CCD) [32] and DHS for TECS (and its components) and the Automated Targeting System (ATS). SMEs provide guidance regarding their specific information/systems to the TSC and watchlisting standards to their Agencies. In some cases, the SME coordinates the data export to the supported system, provides feedback to NOMINATORS, and responds to inquiries regarding their supported system from other TSC customer Agencies.

1.56.2 Upon the conclusion of TSC's review, TSC will either accept or reject the nomination:

1.56.2.1 **Acccpt Nomination.** Consistent with Paragraphs (7) and (8) of Addendum B to the TSC MOU, if a nomination contains the minimum substantive derogatory criteria and the minimum identifying information, TSC will create a TSDB record, include the TERRORIST IDENTIFIERS from the TIDE record, and export the TSDB record to its supported systems (i.e., databases and systems eligible to receive records from the TSDB) for the benefit of SCREENERS that conduct TERRORISM screening. The current supported systems include, but are not limited to, the following:
1.56.2.1.1 NCIC/KSTF;
1.56.2.1.2 DOS Consular Lookout and Support System (CLASS)-VISA and CCD;
1.56.2.1.3 DHS Watchlisting Service (WLS) (e.g., TECS, ATS, Secure Flight);
1.56.2.1.4 TSA Transportation Security Vetting Center;
1.56.2.1.5 TSA-Office of Intelligence Analysis (01 A);
1.56.2.1.6 Tipoff United States Canada (TUSCAN);
1.56.2.1.7 Tipoff Australia Counterterrorism Information Control System (TACTICS).

1.56.2.2 **Reject Nomination.** If a nomination lacks either the minimum substantive derogatory criteria or the minimum identifying information, and is not an exception to those requirements (e.g., TIDE Category Codes 50 or 99 as described in Paragraph 1.53.2), TSC will reject the nomination and notify NCTC directly of its determination or coordinate with NCTC to notify the NOMINATOR of its determination. Records nominated to TIDE that are ineligible for TERRORIST watchlisting may remain in TIDE until additional information is obtained to warrant either watchlisting or removal from TIDE. NCTC analysts will review all-source information for additional identifying or substantive DEROGATORY INFORMATION. If additional information is discovered, NCTC will enhance the TIDE record and submit the record to TSC for inclusion in the TSDB. The TIDE record will be reviewed again by the TSC to determine whether it is eligible for watchlisting in TSDB and export to certain supported screening systems.[33]

1.57 The number of TSC's supported systems will continue to grow as TSC, DHS, and DOS expand their domestic and international outreach efforts and finalize additional agreements to exchange TERRORISM SCREENING INFORMATION. TSC has modified the TSDB so that certain customers may query the TSDB remotely instead of receiving exports of TSDB data to their own systems.

1.58 **Expedited Nomination Procedures for Individual Nominations.** If exigent circumstances exist (imminent travel and/or threat) where an individual nomination into the TSDB needs to be expedited after normal duty hours, a NOMINATOR, with coordination from NCTC, may contact the TSC's TSOC directly. If a NOMINATOR coordinated with NCTC, the nomination will be received by the TSC via the SRQ in TSDB and the TSOC Watch Commander will coordinate with a NDIU Senior Analyst to process the nomination. A NOMINATOR may also contact the TSC directly and provide all relevant information using the following process:

> 1.58.1 The NOMINATOR must first contact the TSOC at 866-xxx-xxxx (toll free number) or at 571-xxxx

> 1.58.2 The NOMINATOR will be instructed by a TSOC Specialist on how to telephonically complete a Terrorist Screening Center Expedited Nomination Request Form.

> 1.58.3 In addition to basic identifying information, the NOMINATOR will be requested to provide a 24/7 point of contact should the KNOWN or SUSPECTED TERRORIST be encountered by a SCREENER.

> 1.58.4 Within 72 hours of contacting the TSOC, the NOMINATOR must provide appropriate follow-up documentation that articulates, through either classified or unclassified means, the substantive DEROGATORY INFORMATION used to establish the basis for TERRORIST watchlisting.

1.59 **Expedited Nomination Procedures for Temporary, Threat-Based Categories.** This provision is intended to enable categories of individuals to be temporarily upgraded in watchlist status based on current and credible intelligence information or a particular threat stream that indicates a certain category of individuals may be used to conduct an act of domestic or international TERRORISM. This temporary, threat-based expedited upgrade (TBU) is made at the direction of the Assistant to the President for Homeland Security and Counterterrorism or his/her designee (Appropriate Official) and should be narrowly tailored to address the threat.

> 1.59.1 The goal of this provision is to fashion a watchlisting response that is appropriate to the nature, specificity, and severity of the threat. To achieve this goal, in addition to verifying the credibility of the threat intelligence, due consideration should be given to:

> > 1.59.1.1 The harm to public safety posed by the threat;
> > 1.59.1.2 The clarity and specificity of the information giving rise to the threat as to time, place, method, and identity of the suspected perpetrators;
> > 1.59.1.3 The anticipated impact on international and domestic travel, civil liberties, and foreign relations; and,

1.59.1.4 The best available screening tools, other than the No Fly or Selectee Lists, given the type and specificity of identifiers and travel data.

1.59.2 When necessitated by exigent circumstances, and where there is current and credible intelligence information or a particular threat stream that indicates a certain category of individuals may be used to conduct an act of domestic or international TERRORISM, the Appropriate Official may direct the TSC and NCTC to place categories of individuals from TIDE or TSDB on the No Fly List, Selectee List, or into the TSDB for up to 72 hours before concurrence is obtained from the Deputies or Principals Committee. To the extent practicable, the initial direction to NCTC and TSC from the Appropriate Official will be in writing. Absent DEROGATORY INFORMATION supporting individual nomination or watchlist upgrade, if written concurrence is not obtained within 72 hours of the initial direction to TSC and NCTC, the TSC will automatically remove any individuals added to the No Fly List, Selectec List, or TSDB pursuant to the TBU, until such written direction is received.

1.59.3 The addition of categories of individuals to the No Fly List, Selectee List, or TSDB pursuant to Paragraph 1.59.2 shall be effected for a period of time, consistent with the nature of the threat involved, not to exceed 30 days but may be renewed for additional 30-day periods upon written approval of the Deputies or Principals Committee. A TBU is valid until the threat no longer exists. To the extent that such threat recedes or is otherwise mitigated prior to the expiration of 30 days or during any extension approved by the Deputies or Principals Committee, TSC and NCTC and members of the watchlisting community shall immediately request of the Deputies or Principals Committee to downgrade these TBUs to their original or appropriate status. All threat-based records transmitted through automated mechanisms (i.e., WLS, CCD) will include a "TBU indicator" at the message level to differentiate this category of records from non-TBU records and to provide the TBU directive for which the record is upgraded.

1.59.4 Until such time as the Deputies or Principals provide additional, written guidance, DOS will defer visa actions with respect to these expedited upgrades in watchlist status.

1.59.5 Departments and Agencies will advise the Deputies or Principals of other consequences that may result from a change in watchlist status and seek guidance as to how to proceed.

1.59.6 After these categorical moves arc accomplished or renewed, there will be an expedited procedure for the review of all U. S. PERSONS that are part of the TBU to ensure their watchlisting status is appropriate (including whether continued categorical watchlisting may be warranted based on the nature of the threat).

1.60 **Arbitration of Watchlisting Disputes.** If a NOMINATOR wishes to dispute TSC's watchlisting determination, it may contact NCTC (for international TERRORIST nominations) to discuss the watchlisting status and/or submit additional substantive derogatory and identifying information to support its initial nomination. Additional information provided to NCTC by a NOMINATOR will be passed to the TSC for review and final watchlisting determination. In the case of an FBI dispute over the TSC's watchlisting determination of an international TERRORIST'S nomination, a case agent must contact the TSC.

1.61 In the case of domestic TERRORIST nominations, if the FBI wishes to dispute TSC's watchlisting determination, it may contact the TSC to discuss the watchlisting status and/or submit additional substantive derogatory and identifying information to support its initial nomination.

X. PROCEDURES TO REMOVE AN INDIVIDUAL FROM THE WATCHLIST

1.62 A NOMINATOR desiring to remove an international TERRORIST identity record previously nominated to TIDE should contact NCTC and provide written justification for the request. NCTC will promptly process the request when received. NCTC will be the final arbiter of whether the identity is removed from TIDE and TSC will be the final arbiter of whether TERRORIST IDENTIFIERS are removed from TSDB.

1.63 If the NOMINATOR requesting removal of an international TERRORIST identity record from TIDE is the only NOMINATOR to have provided information on that record, the removal request will be immediately processed by NCTC. The removal information is then sent to the TSC, which, in turn, makes a determination regarding removal of the TERRORIST identity from the TSDB.

1.64 If multiple NOMINATORS have provided information on an international TERRORIST identity record, NCTC will coordinate with all relevant parties in an attempt to reach a consensus on the TERRORIST identity's most appropriate watchlisting status.

> 1.64.1 If the multiple NOMINATORS arrive at a consensus that the watchlisted identity is not reasonably suspected of engaging in TERRORISM and/or TERRORIST ACTIVITIES, or an applicable exception, the identity is removed from the TSDB and TIDE. In certain circumstances, NCTC may retain records in TIDE to prevent inappropriate re-watchlisting.

> 1.64.2 If the multiple NOMINATORS cannot arrive at a consensus regarding the watchlisting status of an identity, r I SC may decide to remove the identity from the TSDB, but NCTC may retain the identity in TIDE.

> 1.64.3 For cases in which the FBI has conducted an investigation on an individual (independently nominated by another NOMINATOR) and has concluded that the watchlisted individual is not a KNOWN or SUSPECTED TERRORIST, the individual may be removed from the TSDB.[34] In such cases, the TERRORIST IDEN TIFIERS from the FBI's investigation may be used to supplement the TIDE record.

1.65 The FBI will review domestic TERRORIST identity removal requests according to applicable FBI procedures.

1.66 TSC has an established, on-going process to review every record in the TSDB in accordance with Paragraph (8)(b) of the TSC MOU and its mission under HSPD-6 to maintain the most thorough, accurate, and current information in the TSDB. If TSC determines that the watchlisting standards arc not met for an individual record, TSC will remove the record from the TSDB, in coordination with the NOMINATING AGENCY.

XI. REDRESS PROCEDURES

1.67 In January 2005, the TSC established a formal watchlist redress process that allows Agencies that use TSDB data during a TERRORISM screening process to refer individuals' complaints to the TSC if it appears the complaints may be related to the watchlisting process. The goal of the watchlist redress process is to provide for timely and fair review of individuals' complaints and to identify and correct any errors in the TSDB.

1.68 The watchlist redress process is a multi-Agency process involving the DHS, TSC, NCTC, NOMINATORS, and SCREENERS. On September 19, 2007, Agencics participating in the watchlist redress process executed the Redress MOU to set forth a coordinated redress process to respond to individual complaints about adverse screening experiences.[35]

1.69 TSC's Redress Office is responsible for receiving, tracking, and researching watchlist-related complaints that SCREENERS refer to TSC. For each redress complaint received, the Redress Office conducts an in-depth analysis to determine if the person's complaint is related to a TSDB record, including a determination of whether the complainant is the watchlisted individual or merely a near-match to a watchlist record. If the complainant is the watchlisted individual, the TSC's Redress Office will determine whether the watchlisted individual still meets all the watchlisting criteria.

1.70 For each complaint, the TSC Redress Office coordinates with the NOMINATOR (via NCTC when the NOMINATOR is not the FBI), who assists in the evaluation of the complaint to ensure the most current, accurate, and thorough information available is used to review the person's watchlist status. Where appropriate and warranted by the current information and applicable criteria, a person's watchlist status may be adjusted (e.g., downgraded from the No Fly to Selcctee List or the person's identity may be removed entirely from the TSDB). If the redress complaint was referred to the TSC from the DHS Traveler Redress Inquiry Program (DHS TRIP), the individual's adjusted watchlist status will be provided to DHS TRIP for issuance of an appropriate response.

1.71 DHS TRIP is a single point of contact for individuals who have inquiries or seek resolution regarding difficulties they experience during their travel screening or inspection at, for example, transportation hubs like airports, or when crossing U.S. borders. The DHS TRIP website is www.dhs.gov/trip. DHS TRIP ensures a thorough review is completed by consulting and sharing information with other DHS Components and other Agencies, as appropriate, to address the issues identified by the complainant.

XII. PERIODIC REVIEW OF THE WATCHLISTING GUIDANCE

1.72 This Watchlisting Guidance shall be reviewed no less than every two years following the conclusion of the previous review, or as needed.

Notes:
[1] See Appendix 1, Definitions for words or phrases appearing in all capilcized letters throughout this Watchlisting Guidance.
[2] A SCREENER is a Department or Agency that is authorized to conduct TERRORISM screening to determine if an individual is a possible match to a KNOWN or SUSPECTED TERRORIST in the

TSDB. The term "SCREENER" is used throughout this document as a general reference to a government official who compares an individual's information with information in the T S D B to determine if an individual is in the T S D B . Certain SCREENERS have components which perform both screening and law enforcement duties and law enforcement officials w h o engage in such activities may normally describe their targeting or other actions in this context as other than "screening." For ease of reference, government officials who compare an individual's information with information in the TSDB will be referred to in the Guidance as "SCREENERS." The internal guidance set forth herein is not intended to create or confer any rights, privileges, or benefits in any matter, case, or proceeding. See United Stales v. Caceres, 440 U.S. 741.

[3] See Chapter 3, Section V, infra, for more details. Aside from these limited exceptions, references to the T S D B in this Watchlisting Guidance denote the TSDB as containing information about KNOWN or SUSPECTED TERRORISTS.

[4] See Appendix 2, HSPD-6.

[5] See FN 8, *infra.*

[6] See Appendix 3, TSC MOU; see also Appendix 4, Addendum B to the TSC MOU. In 2004, the Secretaries of State, Treasury, and Defense also became signatories to the Memorandum of Understanding between the Intelligence Community, Federal Law Enforcement Agencies, and the Department of Homeland Security Concerning Information Sharing, dated March 4, 2003 (Information Sharing MOU). By doing so, they agreed that all provisions of the TSC MOU and the Information Sharing MOU apply to all entities that are or become a part of their respective Departments. Addendum B to the TSC MOU, which superseded Addendum A, incorporates by reference all provisions of the Information Sharing MOU. See Appendix 5.

[7] The TSDB consolidates the U.S. Government's TERRORISM screening and lookout databases into a single integrated TERRORIST identities database.

[8] NCTC initially was created by Executive Order 13354 (August 27, 2004) to serve as the primary organization in the U.S. Government for analyzing and integrating all intelligence possessed or acquired by the U.S. Government pertaining to TERRORISM and counterterrorism, excepting purely domestic counterterrorism information. Executive Order 13354 was revoked by Executive Order 13470 (July 30, 2008) after NCTC was codified in IRTPA section 1021.

[9] In addition to the provision of domestic KNOWN or SUSPECTED TERRORISTS directly to the TSC, the TSC's TREX unit also provides the identities of international KNOWN or SUSPECTED TERRORISTS to N C T C for inclusion in TIDE.

[10] See Appendix 6, Executive Order 13388.

[11] See 50 U.S.C. 1801(c) (Foreign Intelligence Surveillance Act (FISA) definition of "international terrorism"); Immigration and Nationality Act (INA) § 2l2(a)(3)(B)(iii) [8 U.S.C. 1182(a)(3)(B)(iii)] (defining "terrorist activity"); INA § 212(a)(3)(B)(iv) [8 U.S.C. 1182(a)(3)(B)(iv)] (defining to "engage in terrorist activity"); 18 U.S.C. 2331(1) (defining "international terrorism"); 18 U.S.C. 2332(b) (defining "federal crime of terrorism"); Executive Order 13224, 66 Fed. Reg. 49079 (September 23, 2001) (defining "terrorism").

[12] See Executive Order 13353, Establishing the President's Board on Safeguarding Americans' Civil Liberties (August 27, 2004).

[13] See Guidelines to Ensure that Information Privacy and other Legal Rights of Americans are Protected in the Development and Use of the Information Sharing Environment (December, 2006).

[14] See Appendix 4, Addendum B to the TSC MOU.

[15] The First Amendment does not apply to non-u.S. PERSONS outside the United States. Before submitting nominations, NOMINATORS may consult with their Department or Agency counsel to determine whether a specific person is a U.S. PERSON and whether the questioned activity is entitled to First Amendment protection.

[16] See Appendix 8, Redress MOU.

[17] See Appendix 4, Addendum B to the TSC MOU.

[18] Please note that there are also certain exceptions to the minimum biographic information and minimum substantive derogatory criteria required for Terrorist Watchlist nominations that support immigration and visa screening activities conducted by DHS and DOS. See Chapter 2, Section 111 and Chapter 3, Section V.

[19] See 50 U.S.C. §404o.

[20] EMA is an application used by the TSC to administer ENCOUNTER information.

[21] The Terrorist Screening Database Annex D to the FBI Memorandum of Understanding with Department of Defense (DoD), signed February 22, 2012, established DoD as a screening agency customer of the TSC. The dashed line in the latter chart represents that DoD is finalizing procedures to receive and use information from the TSDB for its screening processes.

[22] In May 2010, the Deputies asked that NOMINATING AGENCIES "ensure that nominations are comprehensive and include the maximum amount of identifying and DEROGATORY INFORMATION." In 2012, the Interagency Policy Committee (IPC), in coordination with NOMINATORS, SCREENERS, NCTC and TSC, developed a prioritized list of data identifiers that arc critical to screening and identity resolution activities. This Identity Resolution and Enhancement Tiers document is available on N C T C ' s Watchlisting Community of Interest portal on the Joint Worldwide Intelligence Communications System (JWICS).

[23] See Appendix 3 , TSC MOU.

[24] PURELY DOMESTIC TERRORISM INFORMATION is provided dircctly to TSC by the FBI and is subject to the same conditions applicable to the nomination procedures for those associated with international TERRORISM.

[25] See Executive Order 12333, as amended, and 5 U.S.C. 552a(cX7).

[26] See I N A § 101(a)(3) [8 U.S.C. 1101(a)(3)].

[27] See Appendix 7 , DOJ Protocol on Terrorist Nominations.

[28] TIDE records for non-U.S. citizens, including LPRs, with insufficient DEROGATORY INFORMATION to meet the REASONABLE SUSPICION standard (TIDE Category Code 99) and records relating to an individual who has a defined relationship with the KNOWN or SUSPECTED TERRORIST, but whose involvement with the KNOWN or SUSPECTED TERRORIST'S activities is unknown (TIDE Category Code 50) are exported to the TSDB as TSDB exceptions to the REASONABLE SUSPICION standard. Additionally, individuals described by sources as "TERRORISTS", "extremists", "jihadists", "militants", "mujahideen" or "insurgents" (TIDE Category Code 03, also referred to as a "labels plus" nomination) will be accepted into the TSDB as exceptions for export to DHS and DOS for immigration and border processing. See Paragraph 3.14.6. A complete list of TIDE Category Codes can found under the "Watchlisting Criteria Guidance" section on the Intelink website at http://www.intelink.gov/tsc/leizal.htm.

[29] "Any alien who . . . . is the spouse or child of an alien who is inadmissible under this subparagraph, if the activity causing the alien to be found inadmissible occurred within the last 5 years, is inadmissible." See INA § 212(a)(3)(B)(i)(IX)|8 U.S.C. 1182(a)(3)(B)(i)(lX)].

[30] Certain categories of non-TERRORIST records (see Paragraph 1.53.2) or nominations to the No Fly and Selectee List based on an expedited waiver of " full date of birth" requirement (see Paragraph 4.18) may also be eligible for inclusion in the TSDB.

[31] See Chapter 1, Section VIII, supra.

[32] CCD is an application used by DOS to administer its visa and passport applications.

[33] See Paragraph 1.24.2 supra.

[34] After an FBI determination that the individual is not a KNOWN or SUSPECTED TERRORIST, NCTC may determine-based on a NOMINATOR'S independent nomination- that the individual should remain in TIDE as records that have been fully vetted and should not be screened against (TIDE Category Code 140), the individual be watchlisted based upon the NOMINATOR'S independent

determination that the individual is a KNOWN or SUSPECTED TERRORIST or that the individual warrants watchlisting based upon an exception to the REASONABLE SUSPICION standard.
[35] *See Appendix 8, Redress MOU; see also FN 16, supra.*

CHAPTER 2: MINIMUM IDENTIFYING CRITERIA

I. BIOMETRIC NOMINATIONS

2.1 Biometric information refers to the measurable biological (anatomical or physiological) and behavioral characteristics that can be used for recognition. Examples include facial photographs, fingerprints, iris scans, digital images, latent prints, DNA and gait. A biometric is sufficient to meet the minimum identifying criteria for nominations to the NCTC's TIDE and/or the TSC's TSDB, provided that the nomination also meets the minimum substantive derogatory criteria, or one of the exceptions. Biometric nominations without minimum biographic information will be provided only to those SCREENERS that have the technical capability to screen against or otherwise make assessments using the biometrics. Notwithstanding the above, all NOMINATORS are encouraged to include all available associated biographic information with any biométrie nomination.

II. MINIMUM BIOGRAPHIC NOMINATION REQUIREMENT

2.2 **TIDE.** NOMINATORS shall provide NCTC, for inclusion into TIDE, FRAGMENTARY INFORMATION that suggests an individual may have a nexus to TERRORISM and/or TERRORIST ACTIVITIES and any additional information that will facilitate identification of these individuals. Nominations to TIDE under this section will be considered for inclusion in the TSDB if the NOMINATING AGENCY believes there is REASONABLE SUSPICION to believe that the individual is a KNOWN or SUSPECTED TERRORIST.

> 2.2.1 Nominations of individuals based on FRAGMENTARY INFORMATION who fail to meet the minimum identifying criteria for nomination to TSDB should be provided to NCTC for inclusion in TIDE when there is DEROGATORY INFORMATION suggesting that the individual is associated with TERRORISM and the NOMINATING AGENCY determines that there are sufficient identifiers for possibly facilitating a match to existing TIDE records. Unless otherwise directed, NOMINATING AGENCIES should prioritize the nominations of individuals who satisfy the minimum identifying criteria before addressing nominations based on FRAGMENTARY INFORMATION.

2.3 **SCREENER Discretion.** As appropriate, SCREENERS have the discretion to decide not to include in their screening systems common names received from the TSDB, where insufficient identifying information exists for identification.

2.4 **TSDB.** Nominations to the TSDB must include a last name, NOMINATING AGENCIES should also provide any additional identifying information available. In addition to a last name, nominations must include:

> 2.4.1 **first name;**
>
> 2.4.2 Or any **one** of the following additional identifiers:
>> 2.4.2.1 Full date of birth (eight digit "mm/dd/yyyy" format);

2.4.2.2 Passport number (with or without country of issuance);
2.4.2.3 Unique identifying numbers such as alien registration numbers, visa numbers, and social security numbers;
2.4.2.4 Telephone number(s) [36];
2.4.2.5 E-mail address(es)[37];
2.4.2.6 License plate number(s).

2.4.3 Or any **two** of the following additional identifiers [38]:
2.4.3.1 Country of citizenship, if different from place of birth;
2.4.3.2 Place of birth (city or country), if different from country of citizenship;
2.4.3.3 Circa or partial date of birth (partial: e.g., 1960; or range: e.g., 1960-1965);
2.4.3.4 Full name of an immediate family member (e.g., parent, spouse, sibling, or children);
2.4.3.5 Occupation or current employer;
2.4.3.6 Specific degrees received;
2.4.3.7 Schools attended;
2.4.3.8 Physical identifiers such as race, height, or weight;
2.4.3.9 Unique physical identifiers such as scars, marks or tattoos;
2.4.3.10 Street address or other sufficiently specific location information.

III. MINIMUM BIOGRAPHIC INFORMATION REQUIRED FOR EXCEPTIONS TO THE MINIMUM SUBSTANTIVE DEROGATORY STANDARDS FOR TERRORIST WATCHLISTING

2.5 There are certain exceptions to the minimum substantive derogatory standards for TERRORIST watchlisting that support immigration and visa screening activities by DI IS and DOS.[39]Examples of these categories of records include, but may not be limited to, records relating to an individual who has a defined relationship with the KNOWN or SUSPECTED TERRORIST, but whose involvement with the KNOWN or SUSPECTED TERRORIST'S activities is unknown (TIDE Category Code 50) and those with insufficient DEROGATORY INFORMATION TO meet the REASONABLE SUSPICION standard for watchlisting (TIDE Category Code 99).

2.6 NOMINATING AGENCIES should provide all additional identifying information available. All nominations under this section must include a full name (first name, last name) and one of the following identifiers:

2.6.1 Full date of birth;

2.6.2 Full passport number (with or without country of issuance);

2.6.3 Unique identifying numbers such as alien registration numbers, visa numbers, and social security account numbers;

2.6.4 Telephone number(s);

2.6.5 Email address(es);

2.6.6 License plate number(s);

2.6.7 Biometrics, such as facial image, iris scans or fingerprints.

Notes:

[36] Only unclassified phone numbers that are authorized for passage to TSC pursuant to Paragraph 7(m) of Addendum B to the TSC MOU, will be included in TSDB. See Appendix 4. Unclassified phone numbers will only be provided to those SCREENERS that have the technical capability to receive this data.

[37] Only unclassified email addresses that are authorized for passage to TSC pursuant to Paragraph 7(m) of Addendum B of the TSC MOU will be included in TSDB. See Appendix 4. Unclassified email addresses will only be provided to those SCREENERS that have the technical capability to receive this data.

[38] As required here, there must be two distinct identifiers that must be sufficiently specific to account for the large number of possible matches common identifiers may produce. For example, if one identifier is rather common (e.g., physical identifiers), the other identifier must be more specific to pemiit the screening official to successfully match a record with an individual. As a further example, a nomination with the last name listed as Khan, location listed as Kabul, Afghanistan, and occupation listed as a baker alone would be insufficient for screening purposes because it is highly unlikely a successful match could be made against such data. However, a nomination with the name listed as R. Khan, location listed as residence of 123 Sunshine Street, Kabul, Afghanistan, and occupation listed as a baker at ABC Bakery, would be sufficient for screening purposes.

[39] See Chapter 3, Section V.

CHAPTER 3: MINIMUM SUBSTANTIVE DEROGATORY CRITERIA

I. INTRODUCTION AND PURPOSE

3.1 TSC issued an updated U.S. Government Protocol Regarding Terrorist Nominations on February 25, 2009, that included an appendix identifying the minimum substantive derogatory criteria for acceptance of KNOWN or SUSPECTED TERRORIST nominations into the TSDB. Based on the attempted terror attack of December 25, 2009, the Watchlisting Guidance was reviewed to determine whether adjustments were needed. The revised guidance was approved by the White House Deputies Committee on May 25, 2010 and issued to the watchlisting community on July 16, 2010, after a multi-agency classification review.

3.2 This Chapter of the Watchlisting Guidance has been updated to reflect the watchlisting community's experiences with the Guidance since issuance in July of 2010 by the Deputies Committee. One of the more notable changes of this updated version of the Watchlisting Guidance is the restructuring of instances for when PARTICULARIZED DEROGATORY INFORMATION is required. Another notable change includes the re-introduction of guidance relative to the TERRORIST facilitators or supporters from an earlier version of the Watchlisting Guidance and the inclusion of additional exceptions to the minimum substantive derogatory standards for TERRORIST watchlisting that support immigration and visa screening activities of the DOS and DHS.

II. REASONABLE SUSPICION

3.3 For purposes of watchlisting an individual to the TSDB, the NOMINATOR should determine whether there is REASONABLE SUSPICION that an individual is a KNOWN or SUSPECTED TERRORIST.[40]

3.4 **REASONABLE SUSPICION.** To meet the REASONABLE SUSPICION Standard, the NOMINATOR, based on the totality of the circumstances, must rely upon articulable intelligence or information which, taken together with rational inferences from those facts, reasonably warrants a determination that an individual is known or suspected to be or has been knowingly engaged in conduct constituting, in preparation for, in aid of, or related to TERRORISM and/or TERRORIST ACTIVITIES. There must be an objective factual basis for the NOMINATOR to believe that the individual is a KNOWN or SUSPECTED TERRORIST. Mere guesses or hunches are not sufficient to constitute a REASONABLE SUSPICION that an individual is a KNOWN or SUSPECTED TERRORIST. Reporting of suspicious activity alone that does not meet the REASONABLE SUSPICION standard set forth herein is not a sufficient basis to watchlist an individual. The facts, however, given fair consideration, should sensibly lead to the conclusion that an individual is, or has, engaged in TERRORISM and/or TERRORIST ACTIVITIES.

3.5 **Due Weight.** In determining whether a REASONABLE SUSPICION exists, due weight should be given to the specific reasonable inferences that a NOMINATOR is entitled to draw from the facts in light of his/her experience and not on unfounded suspicions or hunches. Although irrefutable evidence or concrete facts are not neccssary, to be reasonable, suspicion should be as clear and as fully developed as circumstances permit. For additional guidance regarding the nomination of U.S. PERSONS, see Paragraph 3.15.

3.6 NOMINATORS shall not nominate an individual based on source reporting that NOMINATING personnel identify as, or know to be, unreliable or not credible. Single source information, including but not limited to "walk-in", "write-in", or postings on social media sites, however, should not automatically be discounted merely because of the manner in which it was received. Instead, the NOMINATING AGENCY should evaluate the credibility of the source, as well as the nature and specificity of the information, and nominate even if that source is uncorroborated, assuming the information supports a REASONABLE SUSPICION that the individual is a KNOWN or SUSPECTED TERRORIST or there is another basis for watchlisting the individual.

3.7 **Criteria and Data Quality.** To demonstrate that the nomination has sufficient indicia of reliability to support a REASONABLE SUSPICION determination, NOMINATING AGENCIES should incorporate processes designed to ensure that nominations are free of errors, and to the extent possible given the nature of the reporting, have not come from sources known or determined to be unreliable. NOMINATING AGENCIES should, to the extent possible, verify the accuracy and reliability of the information included in nominations. In addition to ensuring that nominations are free from errors, NOMINATING AGENCIES should implement procedures designed to ensure that recalled or revised information is reviewed regularly, and that necessary corrections to nominations based on those revisions/retractions are made.

3.8 **PARTICULARIZED DEROGATORY INFORMATION.** PARTICULARIZED DEROGATORY INFORMATION is the type of information relied on to determine whether REASONABLE SUSPICION is met. This is information that demonstrates the nature of an individual's or group's association with TERRORISM and/or TERRORIST ACTIVITIES that is descriptive and specific to an event or activity, and is more than a label. For example, "Subject X provides false travel documentation for Al-Qaida operatives" is PARTICULARIZED DEROGATORY INFORMATION, whereas "Subject Y is a supporter," standing alone, is not considered PARTICULARIZED DEROGATORY INFORMATION.

3.9 **Potential Behavioral Indicators.** In making a REASONABLE SUSPICION determination, NOMINATORS should consider behavioral indicators known to be associated with particular KNOWN or SUSPECTED TERRORISTS. The following is a list or a few examples of those indicators. It is not an exclusive list and it includes activity that may have innocent explanations wholly unrelated to TERRORISM. Furthermore, some activities conducted by U.S. PERSONS or activities taking place within the United States, may be an exercise of rights guaranteed by the First Amendment. Watchlisting an individual for engaging solely in constitutionally protected activities is prohibited.[41] For these reasons, it is critical that each of these activities—as with all possible indicators of TERRORIST ACTIVITY—not be judged in isolation. Each must be viewed in the context in which it occurs and considered in combination with all other known information to ensure that any nomination based in whole or in part on this behavior comports with the standards set forth above:

3.9.1 Attendance at training camps known to the IC as facilitating TERRORIST ACTIVITIES[42];

3.9.2 Attendance at schools/institutions identified by the IC as teaching an ideology that includes the justification of the unlawful use of violence or violent extremism;

3.9.3 Repeated contact with individuals identified by the IC as teaching or espousing an ideology that includes the justification of the unlawful use of violence or violent extremism; or,

3.9.4 Travel for no known lawful or legitimate purpose to a locus of TERRORIST ACTIVITY.

III.KNOWN TERRORISTS

3.10 **Definitions.**

3.10.1 **KNOWN TERRORIST.** A KNOWN TERRORIST is an individual whom the U.S. Government knows is engaged, has been engaged, or who intends to engage in TERRORISM and/or TERRORIST ACTIVITY, including an individual (a) who has been charged, arrested, indicted, or convicted for a crime related to TERRORISM by U.S. Government or foreign government authorities; or (b) identified as a TERRORIST or member of a designated foreign terrorist organization pursuant to statute, Executive Order or international legal obligation pursuant to a United Nations Security Council Resolution.

3.10.2 **TERRORISM and/or TERRORIST ACTIVITIES.** In general, TERRORISM and/or TERRORIST ACTIVITIES are acts that: (a) involve violent acts or acts dangerous to human life, property, or infrastructure that may be a violation of U.S. law, or may have been, if those acts were committed in the United States; and, (b) appear intended to intimidate or coerce a civilian population, influence the policy of a government by intimidation or coercion, or affect the conduct of government by mass destruction, assassination, kidnapping, or hostage-taking. This includes activities that facilitate or support TERRORISM and/or TERRORIST ACTIVITIES.[43]

3.11 **Types of KNOWN TERRORISTS for Whom REASONABLE SUSPICION is Established by Recognized Authority and for Whom Particularized Derogatory Information is Not Required.**

3.11.1 **Arrested or Convicted TERRORISTS.**[44] Individuals who have been arrested or convicted for TERRORIST ACTIVITY are considered KNOWN TERRORISTS who should be nominated. The arrest or conviction is presumed to meet the REASONABLE SUSPICION standard for watchlisting unless there is reason to believe that the information is questionable (e.g., faulty or erroneous), of dubious origin (e.g., poison pen, source known to be unreliable, or politically motivated) or the result of an unreliable process (e.g., conviction by a court that does not adhere to minimally acceptable due process standards). Nominations should include the chargc, location, and date of the arrest or conviction, if available.

3.1 1.2 **Individuals Identified Pursuant to Statute or Executive Order.**[45] Pursuant to Executive Order 13224, as amended, "Blocking Property and Prohibiting Transactions with Persons who Commit, Threaten to Commit, or Support Terrorism," Executive Order 12947, as amended, "Prohibiting Transactions with Terrorists Who Threaten to Disrupt the Middle East Peace Process," and section 302 of the Antiterrorism and Effective Death Penalty Act of 1996 (AEDPA), the U.S. Department of the Treasury's Office of Foreign Assets Control (OFAC) publishes, updates, and maintains an integrated and comprehensive list of designated parties with whom U.S. PERSONS are prohibited from providing services or conducting transactions and whose assets are blocked. The names on this list include persons designated under country-based and list-based economic sanctions programs, as well as individuals and entities designated under the various Executive Orders and Statutes aimed at TERRORISM. Persons designated under Executive Order 13224, Executive Order 12947, or the AEDPA are included on this integrated and comprehensive list and are 'Specially Designated Global Terrorists' (SDGTs), 'Specially Designated Terrorists' (SDTs), or 'Foreign Terrorist Organizations' (FTOs), respectively, and should be nominated accordingly.[46]NOMINATORS should regularly check the Specially Designated Nationals List (SDNL) as individuals are added and dropped as new information becomes available.

3.11.3 Individuals Identified as TERRORISTS Pursuant to a United Nations Security Council Resolutions (UNSCR) Concerning Al-Qaida and Associated Individuals and Entities. Under UNSCR resolution 1267 (1999), modified and strengthened by subsequent resolutions, including resolutions 1333 (2000), 1390 (2002), 1445 (2003), 1526 (2004), 1617 (2005), 1735 (2006), 1822 (2008), 1904 (2009), and resolution 1989 (2011), sanctions measures now apply to designated individuals and entities associated with Al-Qaida, wherever located. The names of the targeted individuals and entities are placed on the Al-Qaida Sanctions List.[47] Under the UNSCR sanctions regime, the United States has an international legal obligation to prevent the entry into or transit through its territory of designated individuals listed on the Al-Qaida Sanctions List. [48] NOMINATORS should regularly check the Al-Qaida Sanctions List as individuals are added and dropped as new information becomes available.

3.11.4 Individuals Identified as TERRORISTS Pursuant to the National Intelligence Priorities Framework of Counterterrorism. Members of groups (not support entities) that are identified on the National Intelligence Priorities Framework of Counterterrorism, (NIPF-CT) are presumed to meet the REASONABLE SUSPICION standard so long as the group name is not just a regional or activity-based characterization. Neutral associations such as janitorial, repair, or delivery services of commercial goods do not meet the REASONABLE SUSPICION standard.

IV. SUSPECTED TERRORISTS

3.12 **Definition.**

3.12.1 A SUSPECTED TERRORIST is an individual who is REASONABLY SUSPECTED to be, or has been, engaged in conduct constituting, in preparation for, in aid of, or related to TERRORISM and/or TERRORIST ACTIVITIES based on an articulable and REASONABLE SUSPICION.

3.13 Types of SUSPECTED TERRORISTS.

3.13.1 Individuals Who are Acquitted or for Whom Charges are Dismissed. An individual who is acquitted or against whom charges arc dismissed for a crime related to TERRORISM may nevertheless meet the REASONABLE SUSPICION standard and appropriately remain on, or be nominated to, the Terrorist Watchlist. [49] Each case should be evaluated based on the facts of the underlying activities, the circumstances surrounding the acquittal or dismissal, and all known DEROGATORY INFORMA TION to determine if the individual should remain on the

Terrorist Watchlist.

3.13.2 Individuals Identified as TERRORISTS Pursuant to Other Internal Department or Agency Processes. Departments or Agencies that nominate individuals associated with a terrorist group that is not designated by Statute or Executive Order (see Paragraph 3.11.2) or groups that fall outside of the NIPF-CT construct (see Paragraph 3.11.4) must have internal processes to review the activities of TERRORISTS and terrorist organizations. So long as a Department's or Agency's internal process has determined that a group is engaging in TERRORISM and/or TERRORIST ACTIVITIES, REASONABLE SUSPICION can be met for members of the group, or active participants in, that group's TERRORIST ACTIVITIES. Departments and Agencies that use this clause to recommend subjects for watchlisting arc required to provide written notice to NCTC and TSC (an email will suffice) of the Department or Agency's determination. While members or active participants of such groups may be nominated without PARTICULARIZED DEROGATORY INFORMATION, the watchlisting of an individual pursuant to this clause must be based on the determination by a Department or Agency's internal processes that the group is engaging in TERRORISM and/or TERRORIST ACTIVITIES. Neutral associations like janitorial, repair, or delivery services of commercial goods do not meet the REASONABLE SUSPICION standard.

3.13.3 Individuals Identified as TERRORISTS Pursuant to Agreements by U.S. Government Agencies/Foreign Governments for Sharing of TERRORIST Identity Data. The U.S. Government may enter into agreements with foreign governments for the sharing of TERRORIST identity information. Pursuant to such agreements, data will be provided to the TSC for TERRORIST screening, as required under HSPD-6. The Information Sharing and Access (ISA) Interagency Policy Committee (IPC) or an IPC-designated interagency body, will make a determination, country by country, prior to the final agreement on whether the data provided will (1) be presumed to meet the standard for inclusion in TSDB; or (2) undergo the Foreign Partner Vetting Process.

3.13.4 Individuals Identified as Associates or Affiliates of KNOWN or SUSPECTED or TERRORIST Cells or Networks.[50] Individuals who are associated or affiliated with a KNOWN or SUSPECTED TERRORIST, or TERRORIST cells or networks should be nominated when there is PARTICULARIZED DEROGATORY INFORMATION regarding the context of the relationship that gives rise to a REASONABLE SUSPICION that the individual is engaging or has engaged in conduct constituting, in preparation for, in aid of, or related to TERRORISM and/or TERRORIST ACTIVITIES. Neutral associations such as janitorial, repair, or delivery services of commercial goods are not sufficient. Information about the pertinent activities of the KNOWN or SUSPECTED TERRORIST, TERRORIST cell or network should be included in the nomination. These nominations should include context or content to demonstrate the membership, association, or affiliation to the KNOWN or SUSPECTED TERRORIST, TERRORIST cell or network. Individuals who merely "may be" members, associates or affiliates to a terrorist organization may not be accepted into the TSDB, unless the REASONABLE SUSPICION standard is met and PARTICULARIZED DEROGATORY INFORMA TION accompanies the nomination.

> 3.13.4.1 **Inferences that Support REASONABLE SUSPICION.** REASONABLE SUSPICION may be rationally inferred from the context of the relationship with the KNOWN or SUSPECTED TERRORIST. The following factors should be considered when determining whether REASONABLE SUSPICION may be inferred:

3.13.4.1.1 The nature of the activity engaged in with the KNOWN or SUSPECTED TERRORIST;

3.13.4.1.2 The frequency, duration, or manner of their contact;

3.13.4.1.3 A close, continuing, or direct relationship with a KNOWN or SUSPECTED TERRORIST that reasonably suggests the individual is knowingly involved in or willfully supporting the KNOWN or SUSPECTED TERRORIST'S TERRORIST ACTIVITIES; or,

3.13.4.1.4 Other malevolent or illicit factors that can be articulated that would support a REASONABLE SUSPICION that the individual is engaging in TERRORISM and/or TERRORIST ACTIVITIES.

3.13.5 **Individuals Identified as TERRORIST Facilitators.** TERRORIST facilitators are presumed to meet the REASONABLE SUSPICION standard. The nomination should include PARTICULARIZED DEROGATORY INFORMATION concerning the type of "facilitation" involved and the role of the facilitator when this information is known. Individuals who are considered facilitators include, but are not limited to, financial fundraisers, document forgers, travel facilitators, money launderers, and arms merchants. There must be REASONABLE SUSPICION that the facilitator knew that his or her actions would aid in the furtherance of TERRORISM and/or TERRORIST ACTIVITIES.

3.13.5.1 **Criminal Activity Supporting TERRORISM.** If intelligence or information indicates that the individual is engaging in criminal activity related to smuggling, providing safe houses, forging documents, or any other support to TERRORISTS or terrorist groups, NOMINATORS should presume that the individual is knowingly engaging in criminal activity that supports TERRORISM and/ or TERRORIST ACTIVITIES. In these circumstances, REASONABLE SUSPICION is based on the TERRORIST criminal activity and should be described in the nomination.

3.13.6 **Individuals who Incite Others to Commit Acts of TERRORISM.**[51] Inciting an individual to commit an act of TERRORISM and/or TERRORIST ACTIVITIES under circumstances that indicate an intention to cause death or serious bodily harm is considered engaging in TERRORIST ACTIVITY and is sufficient to meet the REASONABLE SUSPICION standard. The nomination should include PARTICULARIZED DEROGATORY INFORMATION concerning the type of "incitement" involved and the role of the individual when this information is known. Normally, speech will not rise to the level of "inciting" unless there is a clear link between the speech and an actual effort to undertake the TERRORIST ACTIVITY. The individual may have incited TERRORIST ACTIVITY, even if a terrorist attack does not actually occur (e.g., because an attempt to commit such activity is thwarted). Speech advocating a violent or dangerous TERRORIST ACTIVITY is incitement if such advocacy is directed to inciting or producing imminent lawless action and is likely to incite or produce such action. [52]

3.13.7 **Individuals Who Solicit Others to Engage in TERRORIST ACTIVITIES.** In an individual capacity or as a member of an organization, any individual who solicits another to engage in a TERRORIST ACTIVITY and/or for membership in a terrorist organization is considered to be engaging in TERRORIST ACTIVITY. Nominations that include PARTICULARIZED DEROGATORY INFORMATION concerning the type of solicitation involved and the role of the individual are sufficient to meet the REASONABLE SUSPICION standard. An individual may fall outside the scope of engaging in the solicitation of an individual for membership in a terrorist organization if there is information that demonstrates that the individual did not know and should not have reasonably known that the organization was a terrorist organization.

3.13.8 Individuals Identified as Sympathizers and Supporters of a Designated Terrorist Organization.[53] Sympathizers and supporters of a designated terrorist organization (DTO) (see Paragraph 3.11.2) may be watchlisted when the REASONABLE SUSPICION standard is met, and the nomination includes PARTICULARIZED DEROGATORY INFORMATION concerning the how the individual's activities warrant watchlisting, as opposed to information about why the organization is a DTO.

> 3.13.8.1 A sympathizer or supporter of TERRORISM should be nominated if the support is operational in nature. If support is merely ideological, the individual should not be nominated.

3.13.9 Individuals Identified as FOREIGN FIGHTERS. FOREIGN FIGHTERS are defined as nationals of one country who travel or attempt to travel to another country to participate in TERRORISM and/or TERRORIST ACTIVITIES, and to the extent possible, the nomination should include PARTICULARIZED DEROGATORY INFORMATION. Behavior that qualifies as PARTICULARIZED DEROGATORY INFORMATION is the travel to a foreign country to participate in TERRORISM and/or TERRORIST ACTIVITIES.

> 3.13.9.1 A person is not considered a FOREIGN FIGHTER when he or she traveled from Country A to Country B for non-TERRORLST reasons (e.g., enrolling in school). Inferences that someone is a FOREIGN FIGHTER may not be drawn solely from biographic facts that indicate a person was born in one country and is found in a different country and suspected to be participating in TERRORISM and/or TERRORIST ACTIVITIES.

3.13.10 Special Consideration for Individuals Involved with TERRORIST-Associated Weapons. Individuals who possess, handle, use, manufacture, sell, or transfer Improvised Explosive Devices (IBDs), Explosively Formed Penetrators (EFP), Radiological Dispersion Devices (RDD), or improvised chcmical, biological, radiological, or nuclear (CBRN) devices, are presumed to meet the REASONABLE SUSPICION standard due to the inherently dangerous nature of these items or when it can reasonably be inferred from the context that there is a connection to TERRORISM and/or TERRORIST ACTIVITIES (e.g., Iraq, presence of other KNOWN or SUSPECTED TERRORISTS, previous attacks on or threats to U.S. Forces).

3.13.11 Targets of Raids Conducted by the U.S. Military or the Intelligence Community. REASONABLE SUSPICION is presumed where an individual was identified as the target of a raid to disrupt a FTO. When an individual is identified by discovery of information found during the course of such a raid conducted by the U.S. Military or the IC, however, REASONABLE SUSPICION is met where the available PARTICULARIZED DEROGATORY INFORMATION explains why he or she can be reasonably suspected of engaging or having engaged in conduct constituting, in preparation for, in aid of, or related to TERRORISM and/or TERRORIST ACTIVITY. If there is no PARTICULARIZED DEROGATORY INFORMATION on the individual for whom information was discovered during the raid, he or she should not be nominated.

3.13.12 **Individuals Identified as TERRORISTS via Documentation or Media Exploitation Efforts.** Any individuals identified in documents or media otherwise captured by U.S. or allied forces or obtained from a NOMINATING AGENCY must have a connection to TERRORISM and/or TERRORIST ACTIVITIES in order to be nominated to the Terrorist Watchlist. REASONABLE SUSPICION for an individual to be nominated from document and media exploitation (DOMEX) materials may be established either by the content or context of the DOMEX, or other sources. Nominations under this section must include PARTICULARIZED DEROGATORY INFORMATION. For example, REASONABLE SUSPICION for watchlisting can be met based on the acquisition of documents/media identifying a person from the counterterrorism operation that targeted the residence of Al-Qaida leader Usama bin Laden on May 2, 2011.[54] Likewise, individuals listed on a roster of an IED cell could be nominated solely on the presence of their name on the list. An identity from a captured passport, however, would only be watchlisted if additional reporting documents REASONABLE SUSPICION to believe that the individual is connected to TERRORISM and/or TERRORIST ACTIVITY.

3.13.13 **LONE WOLVES.** Because the focus is on the individual's TERRORISM-related conduct, "LONE WOLF" TERRORISTS should be nominated when PARTICULARIZED DEROGATORY INFORMATION and their actions support a REASONABLE SUSPICION that they are engaged in, or have engaged in, TERRORISM and/or TERRORIST ACTIVITIES. No present known affiliation with a terror group, organization, or cell is required but prior affiliations, if they exist, may be taken into account for supporting a rational inference that the individual is reasonably suspected of engaging in TERRORISM and/or TERRORIST ACTIVITIES.

V. EXCEPTIONS TO SUPPORT IMMIGRATION AND VISA SCREENING ACTIVITIES BY DHS AND DOS

3.14 **TSDB Minimum Substantive Derogatory Exceptions to Support Immigration and Visa Screening Activities by the DHS and DOS.** The Watchlisting Guidance contains certain exceptions to the minimum substantive derogatory criteria for TERRORIST watchlisting that support immigration and visa screening activities by the D1 IS and DOS to determine whether grounds exist to deny admission of aliens to the United States (including denials of visas) or to deny other immigration benefits pursuant to the INA.[55] PARTICULARIZED DEROGATORY INFORMATION is not required for nominations made pursuant to the following sections. Because the INA defines "aliens" as "any person not a citizen or national of the United States"[56], the INA admissibility provisions also apply to LPRs, in certain circumstances including those described in INA section 101(a)(13)(C)[8 U.S.C. 1101(a)(13)(C)], who are considered as U.S. PERSONS under Executive Order 12333. Consequently, NCTC developed a mechanism in TIDE to identify and distinguish U.S. citizens from non-U.S. citizens in order to further distinguish between "aliens" under the INA and U.S. PERSONS under Executive Order 12333. The following subsections are exceptions to the REASONABLE SUSPICION standard and will only be transmitted to DOS's CLASS (via the DOS CCD) and DHS's WLS to support immigration and visa screening processes.

3.14.1 **Spouses and Children.** Spouses and children[57] of a KNOWN or SUSPECTED alien TERRORIST cannot be considered TERRORIS TS without a REASONABLE SUSPICION that they arc engaging or have engaged in conduct constituting, in preparation for, in aid of, or related to TERRORISM and/or TERRORIST ACTIVITIES.[58] The INA provides that the alien spouse or alien child of an alien who is inadmissible for ccrtain specified reasons relating to terrorist activities, if the activity causing the alien to be found inadmissible occurred within the last five (5) years, is inadmissible.[59] An alien spouse or child of an alien who is believed to be inadmissible under the INA for terrorist activities should be nominated. No additional DEROGATORY INFORMATION (in addition to familial relation) is required for nomination under this scction, if the individual meets the below qualifications.

    3.14.1.1 To qualify for watchlisting, alien spouses and children of a KNOWN or SUSPECTED TERRORIST must:
        3.14.1.1.1 Be an alien (not a U.S. citizen or national), which includes LPRs; and,
        3.14.1.1.2 Be an unmarried child under the age of 21 or a spouse of an alien.
    3.14.1.2 Ex-spouses, widows, or widowers should not be nominated unless there is a REASONABLE SUSPICION to believe that they themselves are engaging or have engaged in conduct constituting, in preparation for, in aid of, or related to TERRORISM and/or TERRORIST ACTIVITIES. Deceased spouses should not be nominated unless they are specifically covcred in Paragraph 3.17.
    3.14.1.3 Once a spouse or child no longer meets the definitional requirements under this section, such an individual should no longer be watchlisted unless there is a REASONABLE SUSPICION to believe that the individual is engaging in TERRORISM and/or TERRORIST ACTIVITIES. For example, if a child reaches the age of 21 and there is REASONABLE SUSPICION to believe he or she was knowingly involved in TERRORIST ACTIVITY by providing material support to a FTO, he or she can remain watchlisted based upon this DEROGATORY INFORMATION. On the other hand, once a child of a KNOWN or SUSPECTED TERRORIST turns 21 years of age, the individual should no longer be watchlisted under this exception because he or she is not considered a child of the KNOWN or SUSPECTED TERRORIST and additional DEROGATORY INFORMATION would be needed to meet the REASONABLE SUSPICION standard.

3.14.2 **Endorsers and Espousers.** An alien who endorses or espouses TERRORIST ACTIVITY or persuades others to endorse or espouse TERRORIST ACTIVITY or support a terrorist organization may be inadmissible under the IN A and should be nominated.

3.14.3 **Incitement.** Inciting an individual to commit an act of TERRORISM and/or TERRORIST ACTIVITY under circumstances that indicate an intention to cause death or serious bodily harm is considered engaging in TERRORIST ACTIVITY. The individual may be inadmissible under the INA and should be nominated.

3.14.4 **Supporters of a Designated Terrorist Organization.** Supporters of a DTO may be inadmissible under the INA and should be nominated if the support is operational in nature. If support is merely ideological, the individual should not be nominated.

3.14.5 **Representatives.** Representatives of terrorist organizations and representatives of any political, social or other group that endorses or espouses TERRORIST ACTIVITY may be inadmissible under the INA and should be nominated. Representatives include an officer, official, or spokesman of an organization, and any person who directs, counsels, commands, or induces an organization to engage in TERRORIST ACTIVITY. Neither membership in, nor association with, the organization or group is required.

3.14.6 TERRORISTS, Extremists, Jihadists, Militants, Mujahideen or Insurgents.[60]

Nominations o f individuals described by sources as "TERRORISTS", "extremists", "jihadists", "militants", "mujahideen" or "insurgents"[61], (an exclusive list) will be accepted into the TSDB as exceptions for export to DHS' WLS and DOS' CLASS-VISA and CLASS-PASSPORT for immigration and border processing when the following four conditions apply:

> 3.14.6.1 The individual is a not a U.S. Citizen or National (e.g., the individual is a foreign national or a LPR);
>
> 3.14.6.2 The context suggests a nexus to TERRORISM;
>
> 3.14.6.3 Adequate identifiers are available to permit identification[62]; and,
>
> 3.14.6.4 The information has been evaluated as being credible.
>
> 3.14.6.5 It is important to recognize that some activities associated with extreme political or religious views expressed by aliens in the United States may constitute the exercise of rights guaranteed by the First Amendment (e.g., the rights to free speech, assembly and religious exercise).[63] Therefore, someone so labeled based in part on this type of constitutionally protected activity, must have other substantive DEROGATORY INFORMATION indicative of TERRORIST intent. As previously noted, nominations may not be made based solely on protected activity.

3.14.7 Additional Derogatory Information Required (TIDE Category Code 99s and 50s).

NCTC will retain a record in TIDE if it is determined that the information pertains to, or is related to, TERRORISM.[64] However, if a record involving an alien, which includes LPRs, does not contain sufficient DEROGATORY INFORMATION to meet any of the aforementioned exceptions to the TSDB's REASONABLE SUSPICION standard for inclusion, NCTC will generally designate the record as a Category Code 99 (the TIDE category code "applied when DEROGATORY INFORMATION does not meet the REASONABLE SUSPICION standard for watchlisting because it is very limited or of suspected reliability but there is a possible nexus to TERRORISM") or a Category Code 50 (the TIDE category code applied when an individual has a defined relationship with the KNOWN or SUSPECTED TERRORIST, but whose involvement with the KNOWN or SUSPECTED[65] TERRORIST'S activities is unknown) , making it available for export to TSDB for use by DOS and DHS for visa adjudication and immigration processing.

VI. SPECIAL CONSIDERATIONS

3.15 **Nominations of U.S. PERSONS.** Nominations of U.S. PERSONS, in accordance with the Attorney General approved procedures applicable to each element of the IC[66], will be made pursuant to the procedures set forth below to ensure compliance with this REASONABLE SUSPICION standard. Nominations of U.S. PERSONS shall be made based on information from sources of known reliability or where there exists additional corroboration or context supporting REASONABLE SUSPICION. NOMINATING AGENCIES will review information on U.S. PERSONS pursuant to procedures set forth below consistent with the nature of the reporting supporting the nomination and the protection of sources and methods.

> 3.15.1 Special handling is warranted for U.S. PERSONS nominated for watchlisting, especially

by an Agency other than the FBI. To ensure compliance with the Watchlisting Guidance that the REASONABLE SUSPICION standard exists for U.S. PERSONS in the TSDB, as well as to ensure proper interagency coordination, a formal process has been implemented that:

> 3.15.1.1 Ensures the FBI is aware of U.S. PERSONS nominated by any other Department or Agency;

> 3.15.1.2 Requires review of the watchlist nomination decision and concurrence by the TSC that REASONABLE SUSPICION exists for watchlisting;

> 3.15.1.3 Ensures there is interagency awareness of all U.S. PERSON-nominations (FBI or otherwise); and,

> 3.15.1.4 Ensures there is U.S. Government coordination in the investigation and/or intelligence gathering on these individuals, including strategies for engagement with foreign partners if required.

3.15.2 NCTC should include in TIDE U.S. PERSONS who are under International TERRORISM Preliminary Investigation by the FBI but who have not been deemed to meet the REASONABLE SUSPICION standard and U.S. PERSONS with a nexus to TERRORISM, but for whom there is insufficient DEROGATORY INFORMATION to support entry in TSDB. These TIDE records on U.S. PERSONS will not be provided to TSC for export via the TSDB unless approved of as an exception to the REASONABLE SUSPICION standard pursuant to Section V in this Chapter of the Watchlisting Guidance, infra, or as part of a TBU pursuant to Paragraph 1.59 of the Watchlisting Guidance.

3.15.3 For U.S. PERSONS nominated by other Government Agencies who are not under FBI investigation, NCTC analysts receive, process, and export these subjects for inclusion in the TSDB, as appropriate under current procedures. As part of the processing, NCTC analysts identify and share these U.S. PERSON identifiers with the FBI's Foreign Terrorist Tracking Task Force (FTTTF) for assessment, and notifying the FBI case agent of the inclusion.

3.16 **Political Figures or Purposes.** Heads of State or other Government officials should be nominated when there is PARTICULARIZED DEROGATORY INFORMATION to support a REASONABLE SUSPICION to believe the individual is engaging or has engaged in conduct constituting, in preparation for, in aid of, or related to TERRORISM and/or TERRORIST ACTIVITIES. Waivers or other appropriate action can be requested from U.S. Customs and Border Protection (CBP) in coordination with DOS to facilitate the travel of a properly watchlisted I lead of State or other government officials to the extent necessary.

> 3.16.1 Watchlisting an individual is prohibited based on political purposes, retaliation, or any other reason unconnected to the REASONABLE SUSPICION standard.

3.17 **Identities of Deceased Individuals.**

> 3.17.1 The TSDB will not include identity information of KNOWN or SUSPECTED TERRORISTS that are confirmed dead[67] unless:

>> 3.1 7.1.1 PARTICULARIZED DEROGATORY INFORMATION supports a

REASONABLE SUSPICION that an existing KNOWN or SUSPECTED TERRORIST is using that identity information; or,

3.17.1.2 A recognized terrorist organization[68] collects KNOWN or SUSPECTED TERRORIST identity information for use by its members in preparing for or committing TERRORIST acts and identity or travel documents (e.g., related to a deceased KNOWN or SUSPECTED TERRORIST of that organization) have not been recovered. "Trusted travel documents" include all documents used for border crossings.

3.17.2 NOMINATING AGENCIES will share information regarding a watchlisted or nominated individual's deceased status under Addendum B of the TSC MOU, section (7)(m) ("Any other TERRORISM INFORMATION that ORIGINATORS specifically provide for passage to the TSC"). NCTC will export deceased status to the TSC, and the TSC will export deceased status to end user screening systems. NOMINATING AGENCIES will mark deceased status information "TIDE Restricted" in cases where the status, because of sensitive sourcing, should not be forwarded to the TSC. TIDE restricted information will not be exported to the TSC. When a nomination is made on a deceased person in accordance with this paragraph, the status indicator within TIDE that is exported to the TSC will be marked to reflect that the person is deceased.

VII. EXAMPLES OF TERRORISM AND/OR TERRORIST ACTIVITIES

3.18 Examples of TERRORISM and/or TERRORIST ACTIVITIES may generally include conduct intended to intimidate, coerce, influence, or affcct civilian populations or government policy consisting of:

3.18.1 destruction of aircraft or aircraft facilities (18 U.S.C. 32);

3.18.2 violence at international airports (18 U.S.C. 37);

3.18.3 biological weapons (18 U.S.C. 175 or 175b);

3.18.4 variola virus (18 U.S.C. 175c);

3.18.5 chemical weapons (18 U.S.C. 229);

3.18.6 assassination and kidnapping of Congressional Members, Cabinet Officials, and Supreme Court Justices(l 8 U.S.C. 351 (a)(b)(c) or (d));

3.18.7 nuclear materials (18 U.S.C. 831);

3.18.8 participation in nuclear and weapons of mass destruction threats to the United States (18 U.S.C. 832);

3.18.9 plastic explosives (18 U.S.C. 842(m) or (n) footnote L);

3.18.10 arson and bombing of Government property risking or causing death (18 U.S.C. 844(f) (2) or (3));

3.18.11 arson and bombing of property used in interstate commerce (18 U.S.C. 844(i));

3.18.12 killing or attempted killing during an attack on a Federal facility with a dangerous weapon (18 U.S.C. 930(c));

3.18.13 conspiracy to murder, kidnap, or maim persons abroad (18 U.S.C. 956(a)(1));

3.18.14 damaging a protected computer used in interstate or foreign commerce or that is used exclusively by a financial institution or the United States Government (18 U.S.C. 1030(a)(1); 18 U.S.C. 1030(a)(5)(A)(i) resulting in damage as defined in 1030(a)(5)(B)(ii) through (v));

3.18.15 killing or attempted killing of officers and employees of the United States (18 U.S.C. 1114);

3.18.16 murder or manslaughter of foreign officials, official guests, or internationally protected persons (18 U.S.C. 1116);

3.18.17 hostage taking (18 U.S.C. 1203);

3.18.18 damage to Government property (18 U.S.C. 1361);

3.18.19 destruction of communication lines, stations, or systems (18 U.S.C. 1362);

3.18.20 injury to U.S. aircraft or vessels (18 U.S.C. 1363);

3.18.21 injury to U.S. diplomatic, consular, military, or other property (18 U.S.C. 1363);

3.18.22 destruction of an energy facility (18 U.S.C. 1366(a));

3.18.23 Presidential and Presidential Staff assassination and kidnapping (18 U.S.C. 1751(a), (b), (c), or (d));

3.18.24 acts of violence against railroad carriers and against mass transportation systems on land, on water, or through the air (18 U.S.C. 1992);

3.18.25 destruction of national defense materials, premises, or utilities (18 U.S.C. 2115; 18 U.S.C. 2156);

3.18.26 violence against maritime navigation (seizing a ship by force, destroying a ship or damaging its navigation systems) (18 U.S.C. 2280);

3.18.27 violence against maritime fixed platforms (an artificial island, installation or structure permanently attached to the sea-bed for the purpose of exploration or exploitation of resources or for other economic purposes (18 U.S.C. 2281);

3.18.28 homicides and other violence against U.S. nationals occurring outside of the United States (18 U.S.C. 2332);

3.18.29 the use of weapons of mass destruction (18 U.S.C. 2332a);

3.18.30 acts o f TERRORISM transcending national boundaries (18 U.S.C. 2332b);

3.18.31 bombing of public places and facilities (18 U.S.C. 2332f);

3.18.32 producing, transferring, or threatening to use missile systems designed to destroy aircraft (18 U.S.C. 2332g);

3.18.33 producing, transferring, or threatening to use radiological dispersal devices (18 U.S.C. 2332h);

3.18.34 harboring TERRORISTS (18 U.S.C. 2339);

3.18.35 providing material support to TERRORISTS (18 U.S.C. 2339A);

3.18.36 providing material support to terrorist organizations (18 U.S.C. 2339B);

3.18.37 financing TERRORISM (1 8 U.S.C. 2339C);

3.18.38 receiving military-type training from a FTO (18 U.S.C. 2339D);

3.18.39 torture (18 U.S.C. 2340A);

3.18.40 developing, transferring, possessing, or threatening to use atomic weapons (42 U.S.C. 2122);

3.18.41 sabotage of nuclear facilities or fuel (42 U.S.C. 2284);

3.18.42 aircraft piracy (49 U.S.C. 46502);

3.18.43 assault on a flight crew with a dangerous weapon (49 U.S.C. 46504);

3.18.44 carrying a weapon or explosive aboard an aircraft (49 U.S.C. 46505(b) or (c); 49 U.S.C. 46506 if homicide or attempted homicide is involved);

3.18.45 damaging or destroying an interstate gas pipeline facility, an interstate hazardous liquid pipeline facility, or either an intrastate gas pipeline facility or intrastate hazardous liquid pipeline facility (49 U.S.C. 60123(b)); or

3.18.46 manufacturing, distributing, or possessing controlled substances intending to provide anything of pecuniary value to a FTO, member, or group (Section I010A (iv) of the Controlled Substances Import and Export Act).

Notes:

[40] In instances where REASONABLE SUSPICION is not found , NOMINATORS should also determine whether the individual should be nominated to support immigration and visa screening by DHS and DOS (see Chapter 3, Section V).

[41] See Chapter I, Section III.

[42] Attendance at TERRORIST training camps alone meets the REASONABLE SUSPICION standard. Note that under the INA section 212 (a)(3)(BXi)(VIII)[8 U.S.C. 1182(aX3)(BXi)(VIII)], an alien who has received military-type training (as defined in section 2339D(c)(1) of Title 18, United States Code) from or on behalf of any organization that, at the time the training was received, was a terrorist organization as defined in clause (vi), is inadmissible. Note also that 18 U.S.C. section 2339D criminalizes receiving military type training from a designated foreign terrorist organization.

[43] TERRORISM and/or TERRORIST ACTIVITIES include acts that the actor knows or reasonably should know affords material support to any individual who the actor knows or reasonably should know, has committed or plans to commit a terrorist activity, to a terrorist organization or to any member of such an organization. Material support includes providing a safe house, transportation, communications, funds, transfer of funds or other material benefit, false documentation or identification, weapons (including chemical, biological, or radiological weapons), explosives, or training for the commission of an act of TERRORISM and/or TERRORIST ACTIVITY.

[44] See Paragraph 3.13.1 for situations involving individuals who are acquitted or against whom charges are dismissed for a crime related to TERRORISM.

[45] These authorities generally authorize the Secretary of State (in consultation with either the Secretary of the Treasury, the Attorney General, the Secretary of Homeland Security, or a combination thereof) to designate and block the assets of foreign individuals and entities that commit, or pose a significant risk of committing, acts of TERRORISM that threaten the security of U.S. nationals or the national security, foreign policy, or economy of the United States. Additionally, leaders or members of a Foreign Terrorist Organization (FTO), an Specially Designated Global Terrorist (SDGT) under Executive Order 13224, or an organization named to the Terrorist Exclusion List (TEL) may be designated as a terrorist organization by the Secretary of State for immigration purposes pursuant to 1NA section 212(a)(3)(B)(vi)(II) [8 U.S.C. 1 189(a)(3)(B)(vi)(II)].

[46] The comprehensive list of SDGTs and SDTs is accessible through the OFAC website at the following URL: http://www.treasurv.gov/resourcc-centcr/sanctions/SDN-List/Pages/default.aspx

[47] Narrative summaries of the reasons for listing individuals, groups, undertakings and entities on the Al-Qaida Sanctions List (where available) can be found at the following URL: http://www.un.org/sc/committees/l267/narrativc.slitml.

[48] Many persons designated under UNSCR 1267 and Executive Order 13224 are or have been engaged in financial support, facilitation, and other activities in support of TERRORISM. They often, however, do not meet the current criteria for placement on the No Fly List. DHS and DOS will review the information provided about these individuals and take actions, as appropriate.

[49] Because the REASONABLE SUSPICION standard required for watchlisting is lower than that required for a criminal conviction (i.e., beyond a reasonable doubt), an individual that is acquitted or for whom charges are dismissed may qualify for watchlisting based on the facts and circumstances surrounding the acquittal or dismissal.

[50] This section applies as well to persons "linked to," "related" and other similar descriptors to a KNOWN or SUSPECTED TERRORIST, TERRORIST cells or networks .

[51] For situations where there is no PARTICULARIZED DEROGATORY INFORMATION, individuals may be watchlisted as an exception to the REASONABLE SUSPICION standard. See Paragraph 3.14.3.

[52] Ashcroft v. Free Speech Coalition, 535 U.S. 234, 122 S.Ct. 1389 (2002); 9 F A M 40.32 N2.5, "Advocacy o f Terrorism Not Always Exclusionary."

[53] For situations where there is no PARTICULARIZED DEROGATORY INFORMATION, supporters of a designated terrorist organization (D T O) may be watchlisted as an exception to the REASONABLE SUSPICION standard. See Paragraph 3.14.4.

[54] Such documents/media, however, still need to be reviewed to ensure that innocent individuals are not erroneously watchlisted.

[55] INA section 212(a)(3XB)[8 U.S.C. 1182(a)(3)(B)] sets forth several grounds for inadmissibility based on terrorist activities, which is defined in INA section 212(a)(3)(B)(iii)[8 U.S.C. 1182(a)(3)(BX"i)J. For example, INA section 212(a)(3)(B)(i)(VII) states that any alien w h o "endorses or espouses terrorist activity or persuades others to endorse or espouse terrorist activity or support a terrorist organization" is inadmissible to the United States. 8 U.S.C. 1 l82(a)(3)(BXi)(VIl)]. All other uses of the term "terrorist activities" within this Watchlisting Guidance that do not specifically reference the INA follow the definition outlined in Chapter 1 and Appendix 1.

[56] See INA § 101(a)(3)[8 U.S.C. 1101(a)(3)].

[57] "The INA defines "child" as "an unmarried person under 21 years of age...." INA§101(b)(l)|8U.S.C. 1101(b)(1)].

[58] The discussion in Paragraph 3.14.1 is limited exclusively to spouses and children; all other family members (including mothers, fathers, sisters and brothers) should be nominated for inclusion in the TSDB only if there is DEROGATORY INFORMA TION that the individual has a closc connection to a KNOWN or SUSPECTED TERRORIST and that connection meets the REASONABLE SUSPICION standard. Absent independent DEROGATORY INFORMATION, records for these individuals may be retained in TIDE for analytic purposes. See Paragraph 1.53.2.2 for treatment of these other family members as "non-TERRORlST" records that may reside in T I D E for analytic purposes but are not exported to the TSDB (known as TIDE Category Code 160).

[59] See INA § 212(a)(3)(B)(i)(IX)l8 U.S.C. 1182(a)(3)(B)(i)(IX)]. While this provision does not apply when the activity causing the alien to be found inadmissible occurred more than 5 years before the spouse or child's admissibility is being considered, the analysis of the time limit's application will be determined by SCREENERS upon ENCOUNTER.

[60] This exception is commonly referred to as "label plus" nomination.

[61] Insurgency is defined as an "organized movement" aimed at the overthrow of a constituted government through the use of subversion and armed conflict.

[62] An adequate identifier is a biometric, or a last name, first name and any one of the additional identifiers listed in Chapter 2, Section II.

[63] See Chapter 1, Section III concerning constitutionally protected activities.

[64] See Paragraph 1.26.

[65] See FN 28, supra.

[66] The referenced procedures are those approved for each element of the IC pursuant to Executive Order 12333, as amended, which states in relevant part, "Elements of the Intelligence Community are authorized to collect, retain, or disseminate information concerning United States persons only in accordance with procedures established by the head of the Intelligence Community element concerned or by the head of a Department containing such element and approved by the Attorney General, consistent with the authorities provided by part 1 of this Order after consultation with the Director." See Executive Order 12333, Paragraph 2.3, as amended by Executive Order 13618 (July 6, 2012).

[67] Subjects are considered "confirmed dead" under the following circumstances:
a. The subject's death became a high profile case in the public sphere (e.g., media footage confirming suicide bombers' deaths, 9/11 hijackers, death of Abu Musaq al Zarqawi); or,
b. Reporting on the subject's death has been corroborated by at least two credible sources (e.g., United States or "friendly" foreign government, fully-vetted asset).

[68] A classified list of recognized terrorist organizations that are known to reuse TERRORIST identity information is available on the Watchlisting Community of Interest portal on N C T C Current.

CHAPTER 4: NO FLY, SELECTEE AND EXPANDED SELECTEE LISTS IMPLEMENTATION GUIDANCE

I. BACKGROUND

4.1 On October 21, 2004, the Deputies Committee established the criteria for the No Fly and Selectee Lists. On January 10, 2005, the DHS released the No Fly and Selectee Lists Implementation Guidance (Implementation Guidance) to provide direction on how to implement the No Fly and Selectee List criteria. The Implementation Guidance was updated and supplemented on July 25, 2006.

4.2 On February 8, 2008, the Deputies Committee approved the addition of a third and fourth criterion to the No Fly List. The Terrorist Screening Center Policy Board Working Group[69] revised the Implementation Guidance on March 5, 2008, to provide direction on how to implement these new criteria.

4.3 Following the attempted TERRORIST attack on December 25, 2009, the President directed that a review of the current No Fly and Selectee List criteria be conducted and recommendations be made regarding whether any adjustments were needed. The Terrorist Screening Center Policy Board Working Group, in conjunction with the Information Sharing Access IPC, recommended certain changes in the lists' criteria and implementation guidance. Those recommendations were approved by the Deputies Committee on July 16, 2010.

II. PRE-CONDITIONS FOR PLACEMENT ON THE NO FLY OR SELECTEE LIST

4.4 Generally, in order to be included on cither the No Fly or Selectee List, two pre-conditions must both be met:

> 4.4.1 **Minimum Identifying Criteria.** Absent a Special Situation as described below[70], minimum identifying biographic criteria consisting of First Name, Last Name, Full Date of Birth are required; and,

> 4.4.2 **Minimum Substantive Derogatory Criteria.** The minimum substantive derogatory criteria for inclusion must be met.[71]

III. NO FLY LIST CRITERIA

4.5 Any person, regardless of citizenship, who represents:

> 4.5.1 a threat of committing an act of "international TERRORISM" (as defined in 18 U.S.C. 2331(1)) or "domestic TERRORISM" (as defined in 18 U.S.C. 2331(5)) with respect to an aircraft (including a threat of air piracy, or a threat to airline, passenger, or civil aviation

security); or,

4.5.2 a threat of committing an act of "domestic TERRORISM" (as defined in 18 U.S.C. 2331(5)) with respect to the homeland[72]; or,

4.5.3 a threat of committing an act of "international TERRORISM" (as defined in 18 U.S.C. 2331(1)) against any U.S. Government facility abroad and associated or supporting personnel, including U.S. embassies, consulates and missions, military installations (as defined by 10 U.S.C. 2801(c)(4)), U.S. ships, U.S. aircraft, or other auxiliary craft owned or leased by the U.S. Government; or,

4.5.4 a threat of engaging in or conducting a violent act of TERRORISM and who is OPERATIONALLY CAPABLE[73] of doing SO.

4.6 **Detainees at the Naval Station, Guantanamo Bay, Cuba.** Any individual who was a "detainee" held at the Naval Station, Guantanamo Bay, Cuba, unless the President certifies in writing to Congress that the detainee poses no threat to the United States, its citizcns, or its allies. For purposes of this subparagraph, the term "detainee" means an individual in the custody or under the physical control of the United States as a result of armed conflict.[74]

IV. FURTHER CLARIFICATION OF THE NO FLY CRITERIA

4.7 **Third No Fly List Criterion.** Prior to the addition of the third No Fly List criterion (see Paragraph 4.5.3), a concern over the breadth of the No Fly List arose when KNOWN or SUSPECTED TERRORISTS who posed a threat to a U.S. military base overseas did not meet the criteria for inclusion on the No Fly List. Despite national interests, the threat to the overseas military base did not involve either civil aviation (as set forth in the first No Fly List criterion) or an act of domestic TERRORISM to the homeland (as set forth in the second No Fly List criterion). "Domestic Terrorism" requires that a subject's TERRORIST ACTIVITIES occur primarily within the territorial jurisdiction of the United States. "Homeland" does not include bases and embassies located abroad. Even in those instances when the IC had identified a KNOWN or SUSPECTED TERRORIST'S Specific target, KNOWN or SUSPECTED TERRORISTS maintained the advantage of operational flexibility. The third No Fly List criterion addresses this specific vulnerability and counters the ability of KNOWN or SUSPECTED TERRORISTS to target U.S. Government facilities outside of the "homeland" (e.g., the October 12, 2000 attack upon the U.S. Navy guided missile destroyer USS Cole while it was harbored in the Yemeni port of Aden).

4.8 **Fourth No Fly List Criterion.**

4.8.1 **Enable Flexibility.** The fourth No Fly List criterion (see Paragraph 4.5.4) is intended to enable flexibility for nominations to the No Fly List of OPERATIONALLY CAPABLE KNOWN or SUSPECTED TERRORISTS who pose a threat of committing an act of international TERRORISM abroad, but who do not meet the first, second or third No Fly List criterion because they do not pose a threat to civil aviation, a threat to the homeland, or a threat to U.S. facilities and their associated or supporting personnel. Previously, the No Fly List criteria did not prevent KNOWN or SUSPECTED TERRORISTS from traveling aboard aircraft, even though they may have had the intent and OPERATIONAL CAPABILITY to commit a TERRORIST act against U.S. nationals abroad (outside of the "homeland") or against a target with no nexus to the United States or its nationals. The fourth No Fly List criterion now addresses these two vulnerabilities.

4.8.2 OPERATIONALLY CAPABLE Defined. An individual is "OPERATIONALLY CAPABLE" if, based on credible intelligence, he or she, acting individually or in concert with others, reasonably appears to have the ability, knowledge, opportunity, and intent or is actively seeking the opportunity to engage in a violent act of TERRORISM consistent with 18 U.S.C. 2331 or 18 U.S.C. 2332b. For example, attempting to obtain an IED would indicate an individual is OPERATIONALLY CAPABLE of committing an act of TERRORISM. However, simply conducting internet research concerning lEDs would not be sufficient without additional activity. Depending on the circumstances, and in combination with other facts, scouting potential targets or traveling for no legitimate purpose to places that have TERRORIST training grounds, regardless of whether the person is presently capable of using an IED, might also indicate an individual is OPERATIONALLY CAPABLE of committing an act of TERRORISM.

4.8.3 Possible Indicators of Being OPERATIONALLY CAPABLE. In determining whether an individual is OPERATIONALLY CAPABLE, consideration should be given to the following indicators regarding ability, knowledge, opportunity, and/or intent:

> 4.8.3.1 Subject has undergone TERRORIST training or been provided some instruction, to include receiving military training by a designated terrorist group;
> 4.8.3.2 Subject has indicated intent to participate in planning/conducting an attack;
> 4.8.3.3 Subject has expressed desire to martyr him/herself;
> 4.8.3.4 Subject is in repeated contact with a KNOWN TERRORIST facilitator who recruits or facilitates travel of operatives;
> 4.8.3.5 Subject is planning an attack either alone or as part of a group; or,
> 4.8.3.6 Subject is associated with a TERRORIST group/cell and the subject is accumulating weapons/explosives.

4.9 OPERATIONALLY CAPABLE Scenarios. The three scenarios set forth below serve as some examples of No Fly List nominations that would fall under the fourth No Fly List criterion:

4.9.1 There is credible information that the planning or preparation for a TERRORIST attack against the interests of the United States or a foreign government is ongoing and there is an indication that an individual is OPERATIONALLY CAPABLE;

4.9.2 There is credible information that an individual is linked with an organization known to target U.S. interests. The actual target may be unknown but indicated to be a commercial facility frequented by U.S. citizens abroad. Intelligence identifies an operational or pre-operational capability of this individual whose cell is planning a near-term attack on a target {e.g., a plot to kill U.S. nationals residing in a foreign hotel or frequenting a foreign nightclub); or,

4.9.3 There is credible information that an individual is linked with an organization known to target foreign governments. The actual target may be unknown but indicated to be a foreign government facility such as an embassy, consulate, mission or military installation. Intelligence identifies an operational or pre-operational capability of this individual whose cell is planning a near-term attack on a target (e.g., a plot to bomb the British Parliament or the March 11, 2004, Madrid bombing).

4.10 **One-Time Waiver Policy.**

4.10.1 TSA regulations prohibit U.S. flagged air carriers and foreign flagged air carriers from transporting individuals, who pose the level of threat required for No Fly status, on regulated commercial flights, including all flights operated by U.S. air carriers regardless of the location, and flights operated by foreign air carriers to, from, or over the United States. This prohibition applies regardless of the individual's status as a U.S. PERSON.

4.10.2 When necessary, the U.S. Government may authorize and grant a One Time Waiver (OTW) to an air carrier permitting the carrier to transport an individual on a specified itinerary under controlled conditions. OTWs are coordinated with DHS (including CBP and TSA), FBI, DOS and DOJ as appropriate, prior to being authorized by TSC. Once authorized by TSC, TSA will review the conditions of transport and may grant the waiver, permitting the air carrier to transport the individual. If the itinerary changes, or the conditions of transport of the individual change, TSA will deny boarding to the individual until such time as satisfactory conditions are present.

4.10.3 **U.S. PERSONS Encountered Overseas.**

4.10.3.1 While placement on the No Fly List does not legally bar a U.S. PERSON from returning to the United States, the U.S. Government has adopted a policy to review all cases in which a U.S. PF.RSON on the No Fly List is denied boarding on a commercial flight bound for the United States to determine whether an OTW may be appropriate. TSC will initiate this assessment immediately, and may approve an OTW in advance. TSA will not review or authorize an OTW until such time as an acceptable itinerary is available.

4.10.3.2 In order to facilitate communication with such an individual, the U.S. Government has determined, as a matter of policy, that U.S. Citizens denied boarding on a commercial flight returning to the United States should be referred to the consular section of the nearest U.S. Embassy or Consulate, which will facilitate communication with the individual, including providing the individual with instructions in the event an OTW is authorized. In keeping with the U.S. Government's traditional policy of neither confirming nor denying whether an individual is on the Terrorist Watchlist, the individual is not informed of his or her watchlist status or that he or she would be traveling under a waiver.

V. SELECTEE LIST CRITERIA

4.11 Selectee List Criteria. Any person regardless of citizenship, who does not meet the criteria for inclusion on the No Fly List and who:

4.11.1 is a member of a foreign or domestic T E R R O R I S T organization[75] (including a "foreign TERRORIST organization" designated pursuant to Statute or Executive Order, as described in Paragraph 3.11.2); and,

4.11.2 is associated with "TERRORIST ACTIVITY" (as such term is defined in section 212(a)(3)(B) of the INA [8 U.S.C. 1182(a)(3)(B)l); unless information exists that demonstrates that the application of secondary screening to such person is not necessary, in which case such persons may be excluded from the Selectee List.

VI. EXPANDED SELECTEE LIST CRITERIA

4.12 The Expanded Selectee List (ESEL) includes records in the TSDB that contain a full name and full date of birth, regardless of the citizenship of the subject, who do not meet the criteria to be placed on either the No Fly or Selectee Lists, excluding exceptions to the REASONABLE SUSPICION standard.

VII. ACTIONS BASED UPON POSITIVE MATCHES TO THE NO FLY, SELECTEE, OR EXPANDED SELECTEE LISTS

4.13 The actions resulting from inclusion on the No Fly, Selectee, or Expanded Selectcc List are generally as follows:

4.13.1 Individuals that are POSITIVE MATCHES to the No Fly Listare prohibited from boarding an aircraft;

4.13.2 Individuals that are POSITIVE MATCHES to the Sclcctee List undergo enhanced screening prior to boarding an aircraft;

4.13.3 Individuals that are POSITIVE MATCHES to the Expanded Selectee List undergo enhanced screening prior to boarding an aircraft.

4.14 Selectcc, Expanded Selectee, and random screening all result in the same operational response of receiving enhanced screening by Transportation Security Officers prior to boarding an aircraft. TSA will notify the TSC of all No Fly, Selectee, and Expanded Selectee ENCOUNTERS.

VIII. IMPLEMENTATION GUIDELINES

4.15 **General Guidelines.** The watchlisting community has developed six general guidelines regarding the No Fly and Selectee Lists that should be rcemphasi/.ed in order to effectively implement the No Fly List and Selectee List criteria. The six general guidelines are:

4.15.1 When evaluating the significance, relevancc and validity of a threat, careful consideration should be given to the extent to which the threat is current, specific and credible.

4.15.2 The Selectee List is not a default position for those who do not qualify for inclusion on the No Fly List and has distinct elements that must be met before an individual may be included.

4.15.3 The purpose of the No Fly List is to protect against acts of TERRORISM; inclusion on the No Fly List has consequences that are operational, legal, economic, and diplomatic.

4.15.4 Except for expedited nominations made pursuant to Paragraph 1.58 of the Watchlisting Guidance, the decision to include a person on the No Fly List or Selectee List must include substantive DEROGATORY INFORMATION that satisfies the aforementioned criteria and thus justifies inclusion on either list. In cases where nominations contain no substantive DEROGATORY INFORMATION, or contain insufficient substantive DEROGATORY INFORMATION, the individual will not be included on either the No Fly List or Selectee List.

4.15.5 In accordance with determinations made pursuant to Paragraph 1.59 of the Watchlisting Guidance, the White House may direct the TSC to place categories of individuals on the No Fly List or the Selectee List on a temporary basis based on current and credible intelligence information or a particular threat stream that indicates a certain category of individuals may conduct an act of domestic or international TERRORISM.

4.15.6 Under exigent operational circumstances, when DEROGATORY INFORMATION may not be widely disseminated or stored in FIDE, individual watchlist status determinations can be made by the Director of the TSC, in accordance with the relevant criteria[76] contained in the Watchlisting Guidance. Coordination should occur with relevant NOMINATING AGENCIES and SCREENERS.

4.16 **Totality of the Information.** The foregoing guidance is neither intended to be determinative nor intended to serve as a checklist. Rather, it is intended to guide the watchlisting community in assessing whether the established criteria are satisfied for a specific record, based on the totality of available information, a current threat stream, and/or the current threat environment.

IX. SPECIAL SITUATIONS[77]

4.17 **Requirement for Full Names and Complete Dates of Birth.** Generally, TERRORIST identities nominated to either the No Fly or the Selectee List must have both a full name and a complete date of birth. Identities without both will usually not be included on either list. Dates of birth shall not be fabricated.[78]

4.17.1 There is, however, a narrow exception to the requirement for full names and complete dates of birth for individuals from non-Visa Waiver Program countries for international TERRORIST nominations. If a non-Visa Waiver Program country[79] has issued a travel document with only a year of birth, or a verified government-issued identification document with only a year of birth, then it is permissible to use only that year of birth. The NOMINATING AGENCY, however, should, whenever possible, specify the type of document containing the year of birth, and the passport number (if the document is a passport). Otherwise, a year of birth alone will not be accepted for nominations to the No Fly or Selectee Lists. The NOMINATING AGENCY has a continuing obligation to attempt to determine the complete date of birth.

4.18 **Expedited Waiver of "Full Date of Birth" Requirement for No Fly or Selectee Nominations.**

When necessitated by exigent circumstances, a NOMINATOR may nominate an individual or individuals to the No Fly or Selectee List with only a partial date of birth, but for whom there is additional identifying information. This provision is intended to enable nominations based on current and credible intelligence information or a particular threat stream that indicates the subject(s) may be used to conduct an act of domestic or international terrorism as defined in 18 U.S.C. 2331 (1), or as a Federal crime of terrorism as defined in 18 U.S.C. 2332b(g)(5). The goal of this provision is to fashion a watchlisting response that is appropriate to the nature, specificity, and severity of the threat. To achieve this goal, in addition to the credibility of the threat intelligence, due consideration should be given to:

> 4.18.1 The harm to public safety posed by the threat;

> 4.18.2 The clarity and specificity of the information giving rise to the threat as to time, place, method, and identity of the suspected perpetrator(s);

> 4.18.3 The anticipated impact on international and domestic travel, civil liberties, and foreign relations; and,

> 4.18.4 The best available screening tools, other than the No Fly or Selectee Lists, given the type and specificity of identifiers and travel data.

4.19 This waiver should be utilized in limited circumstances when extreme DEROGATORY INFORMATION has been identified demonstrating the threat. The waiver should be valid as long as the threat remains.

X. NOMINATIONS THAT ARE INELIGIBLE/NOT SUITABLE FOR EITHER THE NO FLY OR THE SELECTEE LIST[80]

4.20 Nominations based on exceptions to the minimum substantive derogatory criteria contained in Paragraph 3.14, including immediate family members of TFIRRORISTS (i.e., spouses or children of a KNOWN or SUSPECTED TERRORIST)[81] are ineligible/not suitable for inclusion on either the No Fly or Selectee List, absent independent DEROGATORY INFORMATION;

4.21 Subjects of lost or stolen passports or travel documents arc ineligible/not suitable for inclusion on either the No Fly or Selectee List, absent independent DEROGATORY INFORMATION;

4.22 Deceased individuals are ineligible for inclusion on either the No Fly or Selectee List unless they meet the exceptions set forth in Paragraph 3.17, Identities of Deceased Individuals.

Notes:

[69] This Working Group included representatives from Department of State, Department o f Justice, Department of Homeland Security, Federal Bureau of Investigation, Central Intelligence Agency, Transportation Security Administration, National Countcrterrorism Center, Terrorist Screening Center, Department of Treasury, and U.S. Customs and Border Protection.

[70] See Chapter 4, Section IX, for additional information regarding the full date o f birth requirement and applicable exceptions.

[71] See Paragraph 1.58 for expedited nominations procedures.

[72] Domestic acts of TERRORISM are those that primarily occur "within the territorial jurisdiction of the United States." See 18 U.S.C. 2331(5)(C).

[73] See Paragraph 4.8.2, infra, that defines "OPERATIONALLY CAPABLE."

[74] See 49 U.S.C. 44903(j)(2)(C)(v).

[75] Members of a defunct terrorist group are included in this criterion if the person was a member of the group when it participated in TERRORIST ACTIVITY.

[76] Determinations made under this section apply to the No Fly, Selectee and Expanded Selectee List criteria.

[77] See Paragraph 1.59 for a complete discussion of expedited nomination procedures for temporary, threat-based categories.

[78] The dates o f birth o f January 1 (01/0I/xxxx), July I (07/01/xxxx), November 11(11/11/xxxx), and December 31 (12/31/xxxx) are examples o f dates that may be fabricated and as such, should receive additional scrutiny at all stages of the reporting, nomination, and watchlisting process.

[79] Visa Waiver Program countries include a complete date of birth in their passports.

[80] This section can be overridden in the event of an expedited, threat-based categorical nomination procedures, pursuant to Paragraph 1.59.

[81] See INA § 212(a)(3XB)(i)(IX)[8 U.S.C. 1182(a)(3)(B)(i)(IX)].

CHAPTER 5: ENCOUNTER MANAGEMENT AND ANALYSIS

I. INTRODUCTION AND PURPOSE

5.1 This guidance addresses the collection, processing, and analysis of TERRORISM INFORMATION collected by the SCREENERS during an ENCOUNTER with a watchlisted subject. As described below, all information gathered during an ENCOUNTER with a KNOWN or SUSPECTED TERRORIST[82] is referred to as an ENCOUNTER PACKAGE. This guidance does not create any new authorities for the collection of any information during ENCOUNTERS with KNOWN or SUSPECTED TERRORISTS. Rather, it identifies the types of information that a Department or Agency should consider collecting during an ENCOUNTER with a KNOWN or SUSPECTED TERRORIST if it possesses the authority to collect such information, and should share with the interagency community consistent with their legal authorities and executive policy.[83]

5.2 **Definitions.**

    5.2.1 **ENCOUNTER.** An ENCOUNTER is defined as an event in which an individual is identified during a screening process to be a "POSITIVE MATCH," "POTENTIAL MATCH," or "INCONCLUSIVE MATCH," to an individual who has been designated in the TSDB as a KNOWN or SUSPECTED TERRORIST. An ENCOUNTER can be a face-to-face meeting with a KNOWN or SUSPECTED TERRORIST, electronic or a paper-based ENCOUNTER (e.g., the KNOWN or SUSPECTED TERRORIST has submitted an application for a benefit liked a visa, Electronic System for Travel Authorization (ESTA) application, or information is provided to the United States by a foreign government, aircraft operator, or other private entity). Chapter 5 is only concerned with POSITIVE MATCHES, which occur when the TSC determines that information about a subject encountered by a SCREENER matches a TSDB record.

    5.2.2 **TERRORISM INFORMATION.** TERRORISM INFORMATION in this chapter includes purely domestic terrorism as defined in the *TSC MOU* and incorporates the definition found in in section 1016 of the 1RTPA (6 U.S.C 485), as amended. The term "TERRORISM INFORMATION" means -

        5.2.2.1 all information, whether collected, produced, or distributed by intelligence, law enforcement, military, homeland security, or other activities relating to—
            5.2.2.1.1 the existence, organization, capabilities, plans, intentions, vulnerabilities, means of finance or material support, or activities of foreign or international terrorist groups or individuals, or of domestic groups orindividuals involved in transnational TERRORISM;
            5.2.2.1.2 threats posed by such groups or individuals to the United States, U.S. PERSONS, or U.S. interests, or to those of other nations;
            5.2.2.1.3 communications of or by such groups or individuals; or,
            5.2.2.1.4 groups or individuals reasonably believed to be assisting or associated with such groups or individuals; and

5.2.2.2 includes weapons of mass destruction information.

        5.2.2.2.1 **Weapons of Mass Destruction Information.** Information that could reasonably be expected to assist in the development, proliferation, or use of a weapon of mass destruction (including a chemical, biological, radiological, or nuclear weapon) that could be used by a TERRORIST or a terrorist organization against the United States, including information about the location of any stockpile of nuclcar materials that could be exploited for use in such a weapon that could be used by a TERRORIST or a terrorist organization against the United States.

II. PROCESSING TERRORISM INFORMATION FROM ENCOUNTERS WITH POSITIVELY IDENTIFIED KNOWN OR SUSPECTED TERRORISTS

5.3 This section describes the major types of ENCOUNTERS by various Departments and Agencies. ENCOUNTER PACKAGES obtained from a KNOWN or SUSPECTED TERRORIST ENCOUNTER will be processed as follows:

5.4 **Department of Homeland Security ENCOUNTERS.** DHS has more ENCOUNTERS with KNOWN or SUSPECTED TERRORISTS than any other U.S. Government component. The descriptions below provide information for the majority of DHS ENCOUNTERS, although it is not an exhaustive list of ENCOUNTER opportunities or the types of TERRORISM INFORMATION available for collection. When lawful and available, both biographic and biometric information will be collected as part of the ENCOUNTER PACKAGE.

    5.4.1 **U.S. Customs and Border Protection.** CBP ENCOUNTERS occur at ports of entry (POE), between POEs, or at the last point of departure to the United States at foreign airports through CBP programs like Pre-Clearance and the Immigration Advisory Program (IAP). Information available for collection from these ENCOUNTERS may include, but is not limited to, pocket litter, travel information, identification documents, travel companions, legal documents, and other information gathered during interviews and the examination process. CBP receives international travel reservation information of KNOWN or SUSPECTED TERRORISTS for commercial air travel to and from the United States (which may include travel companion information) and international private and commercial flight manifests, as well as, commercial vessel manifest for travel to and from the United States. With the exception of passenger information required by law to be transmitted to DHS prior to a passenger's arrival, most information is generally collected by CBP when the person is interviewed or apprehended. The National Targeting Center - Passenger (NTC-P) and NTC-Cargo (NTC-C) are CBP entities responsible for communicating with the TSC regarding ENCOUNTERS with KNOWN or SUSPECTED TERRORISTS, to include providing relevant ENCOUNTER information.[84] NTC-P and NTC-C also provide a copy of the examination results to the TSOU for dissemination to the appropriate investigating Agencies.

    5.4.2 **Transportation Security Administration.** TSA generally encounters KNOWN or SUSPECTED TERRORISTS through screening commercial aircraft passengers against subsets of the TSDB and during the application process for a credential or benefit in the transportation or critical infrastructure environment (e.g., Transportation Worker Identification Credential

(TWIC)). When an airline encounters subjects who are possible matches to the No Fly or Selectee List, the air carriers arc required to supply the passenger's name and one piece of identifying data (in the form of a government-issued photo identification that contains a date of birth) to the TSA's Office of Intelligence and Analysis (OIA). TSA OIA submits that information, along with information regarding the carrier, flight number, time of departure, and destination to the TSC.

5.4.2.1 Absent an arrest warrant, or unless probable cause arises during the ENCOUNTER, SCREENERS are reminded **that placement on the No Fly or Selectee List is not a legal basis to detain a KNOWN or SUSPECTED TERRORIST.** To the extent legal authority exists to question a KNOWN or SUSPECTED TERRORIST, encounters with No Fly subjects at the airport may provide an additional opportunity to lawfully obtain ENCOUNTER PACKAGE information. For No Fly subjects who have made a domestic reservation, DHS will notify TSC in advance as well as when the No Fly subject presents at the airport ticket countcr. TSC will then notify the TSOU who will notify both the FBI case agent and the airport liaison agent to coordinate the appropriate operational response.

5.4.2.2 For KNOWN or SUSPECTED TERRORIST ENCOUNTERS as a result of an individual applying for a TSA benefit or credential, ENCOUNTER PACKAGE information can include any supporting documents or information collected as a part of the application process. The ENCOUNTER, and any corresponding information, is communicated to the TSC and other Government Agencies, as appropriate through TSA OIA.

5.4.3 **United States Citizenship and Immigration Services.** U.S. Citizenship and Immigration Services (USCIS) interact with millions of individuals every year and ENCOUNTERS KNOWN or SUSPECTED TERRORISTS who file petitions or applications for immigration benefits internationally and domestically. 85 The USCIS official contacts the TSC to report an ENCOUNTER with a KNOWN or SUSPECTED TERRORIST. Before making a decision on the immigration application or benefit, USCIS contacts the ORIGINATOR/NOMINATOR to obtain additional information that may help determine whether the individual is eligible or ineligible to receive the immigration benefit. In such cases, USCIS seeks further information from the record owner or case agent and may seek de-classification of information relating to the application. In addition, USCIS contacts the ORIGINATOR/NOMINATOR to discuss whether the USCIS decision to grant or deny the application or benefit would interrupt or negatively affect any ongoing investigation.

5.4.3.1 USCIS maintains a presence at law enforcement and intelligence Agency entities to further information sharing regarding KNOWN or SUSPECTED TERRORISTS. USCIS maintains information, including the subject's Alien File (A- File) and other records. The type of information that may be contained in USCIS files, including the A-File, could be biometric data (fingerprints and photographs); identity documents; information relating to the application; addresses, as well as family and work history information; immigration benefit application information; and records of previous ENCOUNTERS that DHS has had with the subject. Other SCREENERS — as well as other appropriate organizations who are considering nominating a potential KNOWN or SUSPECTED TERRORIST or who have ENCOUNTERS with a person who is a POSITIVE MATCH to a KNOWN or SUSPECTED TERRORIST— are advised that they can request, on a casc-by-case basis, a copy of the KNOWN or SUSPECTED TERRORIST'S A-File from USCIS if the KNOWN or SUSPECTED TERRORIST has applied for immigration or citizenship benefits.[86]

5.4.4 **U.S. Immigration and Customs Enforcement.** Immigrations and Customs Enforcement (ICE) is the principal investigative arm of DHS. ICE is also the federal law enforcement organization responsible for immigration and customs-related investigations and detention within the interior and at the borders of the United States. ICE frequently ENCOUNTERS potential KNOWN or SUSPECTED TERRORISTS during enforcement activities under its purview. Such ENCOUNTERS are documented within ICE Enforcement and Removal Operations (ERO) via the Known Suspected Terrorist Encounter Protocol and reported to the TSC and ICE's Homeland Security Investigations (HSI). ICE HSI Special Agents frequently encounter KNOWN or SUSPECTED TERRORISTS internationally, domestically, at U.S. POEs, and when KNOWN or SUSPECTED TERRORISTS are the subjects of an ICE investigation. These ENCOUNTERS are documented by HSI Special Agents in Reports of Investigation (ROI). All ROIs documenting ENCOUNTERS/interviews with a KNOWN or SUSPECTED TERRORIST are shared with the IC.

5.4.4.1 In addition, under section 428 of the Homeland Security Act, the Secretary of Homeland Security has the authority to refuse visas in accordance with the law and to assign employees of DHS to diplomatic and consular posts to review visa applications and conduct investigations.[87] ICE, through the Visa Security Program, exercises this authority. Reviews of visa applications and interviews with applicants can result in the encounter of KNOWN or SUSPECTED TERRORISTS, facilitators, and associates as well as reveal previously unknown information relating to KNOWN or SUSPECTED TERRORISTS. HSI personnel assigned to the Visa Security Program, and to U.S. Embassies and Consulates abroad, work closely with their DOS counterparts to identify KNOWN or SUSPECTED TERRORISTS and report findings through established processes. Finally, ICE may encounter KNOWN or SUSPECTED TERRORISTS awaiting immigration hearings who are housed in service processing/detention centers. These detention facilities can document interactions with the aliens while they are detained in the facility, as well as document materials found on the individual at the time of processing. For all immigration and enforcement activities, ICE will communicate with the TSC regarding encounters with watchlisted individuals, and will submit relevant ENCOUNTER information to the TSC.

5.4.5 **United States Coast Guard.** The U.S. Coast Guard's Coastwatch branch screens crew and passenger information on vessel manifests, which are required by regulation to be transmitted to the National Vessel Movement Center (NVMC) prior to a vessel's arrival in a U.S. port. Coastwatch communicates with the NTC-P and TSC regarding any KNOWN or SUSPECTED TERRORIST ENCOUNTERS during this process. The Coast Guard physically encounters few KNOWN or SUSPECTED TERRORISTS, and such ENCOUNTERS could occur from random and regular inspections of vessels and port facilities, ship boardings, investigations, or Coast Guard licensing activities. The type of information available for collection is dependent on the type of ENCOUNTER. The ENCOUNTER, and any corresponding information, is communicated to the TSC through Coast Guard Office of Intelligence and Criminal Investigations. Based on the encountering situation, intelligence reporting will be written to provide situational awareness to the IC.

5.4.6 **United States Secret Service.** Although United States Secret Service (USSS) does not encounter many KNOWN or SUSPECTED TERRORISTS, such ENCOUNTERS usually involve KNOWN or SUSPECTED TERRORISTS with a domestic nexus to TERRORISM. Such encounters can be the result of investigations or for event screening (e.g., National Security Special Events, political events, large scale sporting events). These ENCOUNTERS will be coordinated with the FBI, who will handle them as they do all other FBI KNOWN or SUSPECTED TERRORIST ENCOUNTERS.

5.4.7 **Department of Homeland Security Intelligence & Analysis.** DHS I&A provides end products and analytical reports, which are generally available to the NCTC and the broader counterterrorism analytic community, including fusion centers. DHS I&A works closely with DHS components to ensure non-traditional streams of information are fused with traditional sources of information from other members of the IC to give a complete picture of potential threats to the nation. DHS I&A "connects the dots" for intelligence reporting and ENCOUNTERS of the DHS components, and as such, has limited opportunity for ENCOUNTERS with KNOWN or SUSPECTED TERRORISTS.

5.5 **Department of State ENCOUNTERS.** For DOS ENCOUNTERS with a person who is a POSITIVE MATCH to a KNOWN or SUSPECTED TERRORIST, the DOS unit at the TSC will do the following:

5.5.1 **Visa Applications.** DOS/TSC will upload the electronic visa application from the CCD to the individual's EMA record. DOS/TSC will coordinate with the overseas posts to scan in CCD all other available DOS documents associated with the individual. DOS information about whether a visa is issued is currently available in individual case records in the CCD; DOS is currently investigating upgrades to the CCD's report function that will make the visa decision data more easily accessible to TSC and other users.

5.5.2 **Visa Revocations.** DOS/TSC will upload the electronic visa application from the CCD to the individual's EMA record.

5.5.3 **Passports.** After encounters with KNOWN or SUSPECTED TERRORISTS possessing passports issued by the United States, the TSOC will upload the Passport Information Electronic Records System (PIERS) application forms from the CCD to the individual's EMA record. DOS/TSC will coordinate with the overseas posts to scan in CCD all other available DOS documents associated with the individual.

5.6 **United States Agency for International Development ENCOUNTERS.** United States Agency for International Development (USAID) works in agriculture, democracy and governance, economic growth, the environment, education, health, global partnerships, and humanitarian assistance in more than 100 countries. When USAID receives an application seeking financial assistance, prior to granting, these applications are subject to vetting by USAID intelligence analysts at the TSC. If USAID/TSC finds that an application relates to a person who is a POSITIVE MATCH to a KNOWN or SUSPECTED TERRORIST in the TSDB, USAID/TSC will provide any TERRORISM INFORMATION concerning the application and follow standard TSC procedures for processing TERRORISM INFORMATION, to include logging the ENCOUNTER in EMA.

5.7 **Foreign Partner ENCOUNTERS.** After each ENCOUNTER by a foreign partner, DOS/TSC will ask the respective country for the subject's photo, additional biographic data and any TERRORISM

INFORMATION on the ENCOUNTER Information List gathered during the ENCOUNTER. Provision of any material collected by the foreign partner depends on the arrangement with, and legal authorities of, the particular foreign partner involved. Therefore, gathering and sharing this TERRORISM INFORMATION will be done on a case-by-case, country-by-country basis.

5.8 **Federal Bureau of Investigation/Law Enforcement ENCOUNTERS.** These ENCOUNTERS can be subdivided into three categories:

>   5.8.1 **Name-Based Queries.** Name-based transaction queries by law enforcement personnel (e.g., traffic stops) made to the FBI's National Crime Information Center at the Criminal Justice Information Services (CJIS) Division that match a name in the KSTF (a sub-file of NCIC) are deemed to be POTENTIAL MATCHES. They are routed electronically to TSC for confirmation and subsequent processing as an ENCOUNTER.

>   5.8.2 **Fingerprint-Based Queries.** Fingerprint-based queries submitted for criminal identification purposes (e.g., an arrest/booking) or for civil identification purposes (e.g., an employment background check) are made to the Integrated Automatic Fingerprint Identification System (IAFIS). For POSITIVE MATCHES to records flagged as KNOWN or SUSPECTED TERRORIST records, the CJIS Division's Special Identities Unit notifies the TSC and the FBI case agent (or the Agency that identified the subject as a possible TERRORIST). In similar fashion, CJIS Division's Global Initiatives Unit coordinates positive fingerprint hits from its foreign submissions with the Legal Attaché. It should be noted that IAFIS and NCIC are separate systems that are not fully synchronized at the present time.

>   5.8.3 **National Instant Criminal Background Check System.** All background checks resulting from attempts to buy firearms or to obtain explosive permits submitted to the National Instant Criminal Background Check System (NICS) at CJIS are run against the KSTF. The TSC is immediately notified of all KSTF "hits." NICS consults with TSC to confirm the POSITIVE MATCHES and the FBI case agent to determine whether there is available information about the prospective purchaser to disqualify him or her from possessing a firearm or explosive as a matter of law. Regardless of whether the purchase is denied or permitted to proceed, all available information is obtained and provided to the TSC and, in turn, CTD, as TERRORISM INFORMATION and processed as an ENCOUNTER.

5.9 **Department of Defense ENCOUNTERS.** The Department of Defense (DoD) has force protection, operational capture/apprehend, and intelligence responsibilities and on occasion encounters KNOWN or SUSPECTED TERRORISTS. To the extent DoD knowingly encounters a KNOWN or SUSPECTED TERRORIST, DoD will report the ENCOUNTER in intelligence channels or to the FBI in cases described in the MOU between the FBI and DoD Governing Information Sharing, Operational Coordination and Investigative Responsibilities signed August 2, 2011 where the FBI is the lead. In cases where the FBI is not the lead for the ENCOUNTER, the Defense Intelligence Agency (DIA) will be responsible for providing extracted information from the ENCOUNTER to NCTC via standard DIA national TERRORIST watchlisting procedures, which utilize community accepted standards. DoD law enforcement ENCOUNTERS will be handled in accordance with established law enforcement standards that provide notification to the FBI.

5.10 **All other Departments or Agencies.** Any other Department or Agency that has TERRORISM INFORMATION from an ENCOUNTER will contact the TSC/TSOC at 866-xxxx to arrange a mutually acceptable transmission method.

III CATEGORIES OF TERRORISM INFORMATION FROM ENCOUNTERS WITH POSITIVELY IDENTIFIED KNOWN OR SUSPECTED TERRORISTS OF POTENTIAL INTEREST

5.11 **ENCOUNTER Information List.** The following ENCOUNTER Information List identifies categories of TERRORISM INFORMATION from ENCOUNTERS with positively identified KNOWN or SUSPECTED TERRORISTS that are of potential interest to NOMINATORS, other counterterrorism analysts, or the watchlisting community. The items identified are not intended to be an exclusive or exhaustive list of what constitutes TERRORISM INFORMATION.

5.11.1 ENCOUNTER information identified for collection in Addendum B to the TSC MOU[88] when there is a POSITIVE MATCH to a KNOWN or SUSPECTED TERRORIST:
1. Photographs
2. Fingerprints
3. Pocket litter
4. Written data
5. Reports of TERRORISMINFORMATION

5.11.2 Additional items of potential interest when lawfully collected during an ENCOUNTER with a KNOWN or SUSPECTED TERRORIST:
1. Contemporaneous reports including the impressions or observations recorded by an official involved in the ENCOUNTER:

   a) Reason/circumstances of ENCOUNTER
   b) ICE Intel Reports
   c) FBI Reports of Investigations
   d) CBP Incident Reports
   e) CBP Secondary Exam Report
   f) USCIS applications or petitions
   g) Non-Immigrant Visa (NIV) Applications (including CCD notes)
   h) State, Local, Tribal, Territorial Police Report
   i) TSA OIA No Fly and Selectee Reports
   j) TSA OIA ENCOUNTER Reports (Vetting Match Reports) on transportation workers and other populations vetted by TSA against the TSDB
   k) Spot Reports
   l) Suspicious Activity Reports
   m) Impounded vehicle inventory
   n) Any inventory record
   o) Any pictures, video or recording of or from the actual ENCOUNTER
   p) Biometric or biographic identifiers of traveling associates

2. Surveillance-related documents:
   a) Maps
   b) Pictures
   c) Visitor or site information
   d) Plans or diagrams (e.g., architectural drawings, blueprints, schemas)

3. Context regarding areas of potential interest or possible targets of KNOWN or SUSPECTED TERRORIST interest:
   a) Information regarding any high profile events taking place in geographic area of ENCOUNTER
   b) Any critical infrastructure sites near the geographic area o f ENCOUNTER
   c) Unique characteristics or facts about your domain/area of responsibility/geographic area of ENCOUNTER
   d) Event tickets (e.g., sporting events, concerts, designated National Security Special events)
   e) Building access passes, electronic cards, fobs, keys

4. Mode of transportation used by the person who is a POSITIVE MATCH to a KNOWN or SUSPECTED TERRORIST, along with identifying information:
   a) Vehicle information (e.g., Vehicle registration, Vehicle identification number (VIN), Title, Driver's license, Car insurance cards or information)
   b) Pilot medical license
   c) Pilot certificates
   d) Aircraft registration
   e) Marine registration
   f) EZ Pass or electronic vehicle payment system

5. Travel-related information:
   a) Passport exit/entry stamps indicating places of travel
   b) Any visa application or denial information from other countries
   c) Travel itineraries
   d) Tickets (e.g., plane, train, boat)
   e) Hotels (e.g., reservation confirmation, receipts)
   f) Rental cars (e.g., reservation confirmation, agreement, receipts)
   g) Reservation method (e.g., via travel agency or travel website)
   h) PNR data
   i) Travel manifests
   j) Luggage or baggage tags (e.g., airport check-in tags, identification tags,
   k) lost bag bar code tags)
   l) Claim checks
   m) Storage locker keys
   n) Shipping documents and receipts
   o) Automated Identification System (AIS) information for maritime shipping
   p) Foreign airport security check stickers or labels
   q) Conference/seminar materials (e.g., invitation, brochure, schedule)

6. Information about gold and jewelry worn by person at time of ENCOUNTER (e.g., receipts)

7. General items information:
   a) Business cards
   b) Phone numbers
   c) Address books
   d) Email addresses

e) Any cards with an electronic strip on it (hotel cards, grocery cards, gift cards, frequent flyer cards)
f) Pre-paid phone cards
g) Insurance cards
h) Medical/Health insurance information
i) Prescription information (e.g., doctor, pharmacy information)
j) Sales receipts
k) Any additional biographic or biomctric identifiers to enhance identity matching of associates or family members with a person who is a POSITIVE MATCH to a KNOWN or SUSPECTED TERRORIST (as well as associates or family members referenced in interviews or documents carried by a person who is a POSITIVE MATCH to a KNOWN or SUSPECTED TERRORIST)
l) Copies of identification documents obtained during the ENCOUNTER with a person who is a POSITIVE MATCH to a KNOWN or SUSPECTED TERRORIST (e.g., passports, Seaman's Papers, Airman Certificates, driver's licenses, state identification cards, and similar government identification documents)
m) Any computer, uniform resource locator (URL), or Internet protocol (IP) address information
n) Calendars/schedulers

8. Licenses, permits, membership cards, and application information:
   a) Membership cards (including library cards)
   b) Gun show applications, firearms license, concealed weapons permit, shooting club memberships
   c) HAZMAT license
   d) Explosives permit

9. Tools or equipment information:
   a) Scuba gear
   b) Multiple cell phones
   c) Binoculars
   d) Peroxide
   e) Ammunition
   f) Camping fuel tabs
   g) Any dual use material that could be used for TERRORIST ACTIVITY

10. Financial information:
    a) Check book/individual or loose checks, including cashier's checks
    b) Bank account numbers
    c) Credit cards, especially those issued by U.S. banks and carried by non- U.S. PERSONS
    d) Tax records
    e) Business financial records
    f) Bank statements
    g) Credit card or billing statements
    h) Utility bills
    i) Anything with an account number
    j) Wire transfer information, including receipts from Money Service Businesses
    k) Denominations of money being carried (i.e., what country(ies) currency(ies) are they

carrying), including, if possible, the serial numbers of currency carried
- l) Automated teller machine (ATM) receipts
- m) Ledgers

11. Electronic media/devices observed or copied:
- a) Cell phone list and speed dial numbers
- b) Laptop images
- c) GPS
- d) Thumb drives
- e) Disks
- f) iPod or MP3
- g) PDAs (e.g., Palm Pilots, Trios)
- h) Kindle or iPad (electronic books)
- i) Cameras
- j) Video and/or voice recorders
- k) Pagers
- l) Any electronic storage media

12. Employment information:
- a) Pay stubs
- b) Employment applications
- c) Want ads
- d) Employer correspondence
- e) Access cards, badges

13. Professional papers/Academic information:
- a) Resumes
- b) Acadcmic transcripts

14. Legal document information:
- a) Birth certificates
- b) Immigration and naturalization documents
- c) Marriage licenses
- d) Divorce decrees
- e) Adoption papers
- f) Living Wills
- g) Last Will and Testament
- h) Parking tickets
- i) Speeding tickets
- j) Property records (deeds)
- k) Summons
- l) Criminal documents or civil lawsuit information

15. Miscellaneous item information:
- a) Long term storage facilities (e.g., access keys, codes)
- b) Social networking accounts (e.g., Facebook, Twitter, MySpacc, Linkcdln, ICQ)
- c) Titles of books, DVD/CD, brochures being carried and their condition (e.g., new, dog-eared, annotated, unopened, professional journals)
- d) Letters, envelopes

e) Letters of Introduction

f) Animal information (e.g., vet or chip information)

IV. ENCOUNTER MANAGEMENT ACTIONS

5.12 Handling of ENCOUNTER PACKAGES. This section outlines the processes for handling and sharing ENCOUNTER PACKAGES by SCREENERS, the TSC and NCTC.

5.13 FBI/Law Enforcement ENCOUNTERS. TSOU coordinates the U.S. Government's response to an ENCOUNTER with a KNOWN or SUSPECTED TERRORIST. All collection of TERRORISM INFORMATION during law enforcement ENCOUNTERS (e.g., traffic violations, investigations, arrests) are coordinated between the NOMINATING AGENCY and the ENCOUNTERING AGENCY via TSOU.

> 5.13.1 For domestic and international ENCOUNTERS with a person who is a POSITIVE MATCH to a KNOWN or SUSPECTED TERRORIST, TSOU will do the following: After receiving notification of an ENCOUNTER from the TSC, TSOU will disseminate and coordinate information to FBI operational entities and federal, state, and local law enforcement Agencies. TSOU simultaneously coordinates with the appropriate FBI Field Division(s) and Case Agent(s); Joint Terrorist Task Forces (JTTFs); Airport Liaison Agents and Attaches (ALAs); ;Legal Attachés (LEGATs); U.S. Embassies and/or other appropriate law enforcement officials, including ICE and CBP (specifically, NTC-P and NTC-C as appropriate); and appropriate members of the IC. For outbound ENCOUNTERS, or ENCOUNTERS involving subjects who have certain DEROGATORY INFORMATION, TSOU contacts (via phone and electronic notification) the appropriate counterterrorism element(s). Especially sensitive ENCOUNTERS often require coordination and situational updates with the White House, Northern Command (NORTHCOM), and FBI's Counterterrorism-Watch.

5.14 TSC Actions. TSC will update existing KNOWN or SUSPECTED TERRORIST records with new TERRORIST IDENTIFIERS and TERRORISM INFORMATION and will provide the broader counterterrorism analytic community with as much new information as possible stemming from an ENCOUNTER with a KNOWN or SUSPECTED TERRORIST. TSC's primary methods for sharing TERRORISM INFORMATION with the broader counterterrorism analytic community will be through its EMA application and the use of Intelligence Information Reports (IIRs), as described further in Section V, infra. TSC will also coordinate with Fusion Centers on law enforcement and other ENCOUNTERS impacting their Area of Responsibility. This coordination will include a request for record enhancing information from the Fusion Center, which if received, will be added to the subject's KNOWN or SUSPECTED TERRORIST record.

> 5.14.1 Any new TERRORISM INFORMATION recorded in, or attached to an EMA record by TSC will be provided to NCTC via an automated ingest process.[89] Such daily ingests of EMA records update NCTC's TIDE to reflect the fact of the ENCOUNTER, any new identifiers used to confirm the KNOWN or SUSPECTED TERRORIST POSITIVE MATCHES, or those identified in an IIR. Once TIDE has been updated, an automated ingest from TIDE to TSDB is used to update the various TSDB subsets (e.g., No Fly or Selectee Lists). At this point, the process is complete and the watchlisting, screening and law enforcement communities have the most current and thorough TERRORISM INFORMATION available about a KNOWN or

SUSPECTED TERRORIST. Most—but not all—of that TERRORISM INFORMATION is available in a structured format as part of the KNOWN or SUSPECTED TERRORIST record (e.g., discrete elements such as a date of birth, country of origin). The unstructured TERRORISM INFORMATION, while also in digitized format (e.g., a computer disk, a scanned image of a business card, an encountering officer's report), is handled by NCTC.

5.15 **NCTC Actions.** NCTC will post to TIDE Online any digitized ENCOUNTER PACKAGE it receives from TSC or directly from a SCREENER. ENCOUNTER PACKAGES can be found under the subject's main page.

V. ROLES AND RESPONSIBILITIES FOR UPDATING EXISTING KNOWN OR SUSPECTED TERRORIST RECORDS AND NOMINATING NEW KNOWN OR SUSPECTED TERRORISTS BASED ON INFORMATION FROM POSITIVE ENCOUNTERS

5.16 This section describes the roles and responsibilities of the watchlisting, screening, and counterterrorism communities for exploitation and analysis of the TERRORISM INFORMATION lawfully collected and shared when there is a POSITIVE MATCH to a KNOWN or SUSPECTED TERRORIST. In this context the following definitions apply:

> 5.16.1 **"INITIAL REVIEW"** means a quick review of the ENCOUNTER PACKAGE to identify obvious, new TERRORIST IDENTIFIERS about the KNOWN or SUSPECTED TERRORIST.

> 5.16.2 **"ADVANCED ANALYSIS"** means a thorough review of the TERRORISM INFORMATION contained in an ENCOUNTER PACKAGE obtained as a result of the ENCOUNTER with the KNOWN or SUSPECTED TERRORIST. ADVANCED ANALYSIS includes the adding of TERRORIST IDENTIFIERS to existing KNOWN or SUSPECTED TERRORIST records and identifying new KNOWN or SUSPECTED TERRORISTS who should be nominated through the existing nomination process. In this context, ADVANCED ANALYSIS is being done on a tactical matter related to the specific KNOWN or SUSPECTED TERRORIST to identify information useful in "connecting the dots" between and among that KNOWN or SUSPECTED TERRORIST and other KNOWN or SUSPECTED TERRORISTS or potential KNOWN or SUSPECTED TERRORISTS. It is also when the need for foreign language translation services will be identified.

> 5.16.3 **"TARGETED ANALYSIS"** means further exploitation of a targeted set of ENCOUNTER PACKAGES and ADVANCED ANALYSIS products to assist in identifying TERRORIST trends and changes to methods, tactics, and practices. ENCOUNTERS for TARGETED ANALYSIS are selected using contemporaneous threat criteria and research in additional repositories. Contemporaneous threat criteria includes association with a priority terrorist group (e.g., NIPF Tier I or II); ENCOUNTERS with KNOWN or SUSPECTED TERRORISTS designated as No Fly or associated with violent activity; or at the request of any Department or Agency that identifies a need.

5.17 Results of INITIAL REVIEW, ADVANCED ANALYSIS, and TARGETED ANALYSIS efforts (collectively, "Exploitation") by Departments or Agencies will be reported to the watchlisting, screening and counterterrorism communities using standard templates when available.

5.17.1 **TSC Actions.**

5.17.1.1 **First Stage Review.** TSC actions with KNOWN or SUSPECTED TERRORIST ENCOUNTERS occur in two stages. The first stage occurs when the ENCOUNTERING AGENCY and TSC exchange TERRORIST IDENTIFIERS to determine whether the individual is watchlisted (i.e., a POSITIVE MATCH to a TSDB record). TSC records any new TERRORIST IDENTIFIERS provided during this stage in TSC's EMA application.

5.17.1.2 **Second Stage Review.** The second stage occurs after TSC has confirmed there is a POSITIVE MATCH to a KNOWN or SUSPECTED TERRORIST. For each POSITIVE MATCH to a KNOWN or SUSPECTED TERRORIST, the TSC's Office of Intelligence (TSC/OI) will generate an IIR for dissemination to the counterterrorism community that provides a summary about the KNOWN or SUSPECTED TERRORIST ENCOUNTER (e.g., basic facts about the ENCOUNTER such as date, time, and place). If available at the time the initial IIR is prepared, TSC/OI will conduct an INITIAL REVIEW of the ENCOUNTER PACKAGE and provide a thumbnail summary of the TERRORISM INFORMATION. For example, a summary might highlight the existence of a new KNOWN or SUSPECTED TERRORIST ("KNOWN or SUSPECTED TERRORIST was traveling with three other associates not previously identified in the car where the explosives were found in a hidden compartment") or the possibility that new TERRORIST IDENTIFIERS are available ("approximately 80 pages carried by the KNOWN or SUSPECTED TERRORIST were converted to electronic documents ranging from the KNOWN or SUSPECTED TERRORIST'S calendar/address book to bank account and credit card numbers").

5.17.2 **National Media Exploitation Center Actions.** Much of the TERRORISM INFORMATION generated by ENCOUNTERS from a person who is a POSITIVE MATCH to a KNOWN or SUSPECTED TERRORIST is expected to be in a foreign language that may hinder prompt exploitation. The National Media Exploitation Center (NMEC) has the capability to translate foreign language information and the experience necessary to understand the efforts used to hide their activities. When TSC receives ENCOUNTER PACKAGES with information in a foreign language, or when NCTC receives them directly from an ENCOUNTERING AGENCY, TSC or NCTC will forward/notify NMEC that it has the action to translate the ENCOUNTER PACKAGE. Once the ENCOUNTER PACKAGE has been translated and returned to TSC and NCTC, the assigned roles and responsibility for exploitation will apply.

5.17.3 **FBI Actions.** The majority of the FBI's ENCOUNTERS with KNOWN or SUSPECTED TERRORISTS occur in the United States. The FBI has ADVANCED ANALYSIS responsibility for ENCOUNTER PACKAGES on KNOWN or SUSPECTED TERRORISTS for whom the FBI has an open investigation, no matter where the individual is encountered. If the FBI does not have an open investigation on a KNOWN or SUSPECTED TERRORIST encountered in the United States, or if the KNOWN or SUSPECTED TERRORIST is a U.S. PERSON, then TSOU will send a lead directing the appropriate FBI field office to conduct an assessment of the individual and the ENCOUNTER circumstances to determine whether to open a preliminary or full investigation.[90] This assessment includes ADVANCED ANALYSIS packages when provided by ENCOUNTERING AGENCIES. If no investigation is opened, an IIR will be sent to the NOMINATING AGENCY and NCTC which will be used to enhance the TIDE record with additional FBI-derived information.

5.17.4 **DHS I&A Actions.** DHS I&A has ADVANCED ANALYSIS responsibility for ENCOUNTER PACKAGES where the KNOWN or SUSPECTED TERRORIST is denied entry, denied ESTA, denied boarding, or is subject to a no board recommendation at a foreign location, or identified through ICE's visa security processes.

5.17.5 **NCTC Actions.** On occasion, DOS, USAID, and foreign governments have ENCOUNTERS with KNOWN or SUSPECTED TERRORISTS, usually in the form of a record ENCOUNTER (e.g., the KNOWN or SUSPECTED TERRORIST has submitted an application for a benefit like a visa or grant or information is provided to the United States by a foreign government). NCTC has ADVANCED ANALYSIS responsibility for ENCOUNTER PACKAGES in these instances.

5.17.5.1 For TARGETED ANALYSIS, NCTC offers this capability for a select set of ENCOUNTER PACKAGES based on internal or interagency tasking. Since all ADVANCED ANALYSIS products created by FBI, DHS, or NCTC will be disseminated to the U.S. Government via an IIR, these materials are available to any organization seeking to further exploit specific ENCOUNTERS. NCTC will leverage these ADVANCED ANALYSIS products as part of its typical intelligence analytic process to highlight emerging threats, issues or concerns.

5.17.6 A chart depicting the roles and responsibilities by Department or Agency may be found at the end of this Chapter.

VI. RESPONSIBILITY TO COORDINATE ANY ACTIONS CONTEMPLATED BASED ON INFORMATION FROM ENCOUNTERS WITH A KNOWN OR SUSPECTED TERRORIST

5.18 **Information Sharing MOU Requirements.** Departments and Agencies are reminded of their agreement to provide transparency between and among them with regard to their "activities to preempt, prevent, and disrupt TERRORIST attacks against U.S. PERSONS and interests.[91]" As a practical matter, that type of transparency demands, to the greatest extent possible, prior coordination with affected Departments or Agencies before action within a Department or Agency's authorities is taken based on TERRORISM INFORMATION from a person who is a POSITIVE MATCH to a KNOWN or SUSPECTED TERRORIST. For example, FBI, Central Intelligence Agency (CIA) or DOD, as lead counterterrorism Agencies in their respective domains, must be consulted prior to taking any action based on ENCOUNTERS with a person who is a POSITIVE MATCH with KNOWN or SUSPECTED TERRORIST. This guidance is subject to existing policies and coordination procedures when action against or pertaining to the KNOWN or SUSPECTED TERRORIST is contemplated.

5.19 **Requests for Withholding of Action.** In certain circumstances, law enforcement or the IC may request that a SCREENER not take action (e.g., not to refuse the visa, to allow individual to enter the United States, to not deny an individual to obtain an immigration benefit or access to the secure area of an airport) although action may be taken under the law. This request, to the extent practicable, shall be in writing, by a senior official, and include a statement of justification and risk mitigation. Departments and Agencies will establish mutually acceptable processes and procedures to implement a detailed plan.

VII. EXAMPLES OF TERRORISM INFORMATION TYPICALLY AVAILABLE FROM ENCOUNTERS

5.20 The following examples of various types of ENCOUNTERS and the type of information typically generated from those ENCOUNTERS is offered to assist Departments and Agencies in understanding what additional or new information may become available as a result of following the guidance provided in this document.

5.20.1 **Ports of Entry.** Types of documents that could be included in the ENCOUNTER PACKAGE typically include:
1. Business cards
2. Copies of passport and visa entries
3. Driver's license
4. Resumes
5. Conference literature
6. Correspondence not in possession of the U.S. Postal Service.
7. Letters of introduction
8. Checks, bank deposit slips
9. Calendar/schedule
10. Address book
11. Notepad entries
12. Mariner's certificates
13. Telephone data
14. Location and duration of previous travel stops on current or past travel itinerary

5.20.2 **Law Enforcement ENCOUNTERS.** Information collected from law enforcement ENCOUNTERS with a person who is a POSITIVE MATCH to a KNOWN or SUSPECTED TERRORIST can include any information that would be collected when a law enforcement officer speaks with a KNOWN or SUSPECTED TERRORIST. Typically information that could be included in the ENCOUNTER PACKAGE can include, but is not limited to:
1. Associates
2. Telephone numbers (home, business, cell, pager, or fax)
3. Other forms of identification
4. Physical descriptors
5. Family members
6. Occupation and work history
7. Travel plans or history
8. Vehicle information

5.20.3 **Visa Applications.** A typical DOS ENCOUNTER PACKAGE with a person who is a POSITIVE MATCH to a KNOWN or SUSPECTED TERRORIST will be a visa application for entry to the United States, which identifies basic information about the encountered KNOWN or SUSPECTED TERRORIST and the ENCOUNTER. Types of documents that could be included in the ENCOUNTER PACKAGE typically include:

1.   Home and work address
2.   Copies of passport and visa entries
3.   National Identification Number (if applicable to the country)
4.   Phone numbers (home, business, cell, pager, or fax)
5.   Sponsorship information (when available, to include individual's name/Company/Government, address and contact information)
6.   Family member names (e.g., spouse, parents, children)
7.   Police Certificates (if applicable)
8.   Biometrics (Photos and Fingerprint Identification Number (FIN))
9.   Resumes (when applying for business visas)
10. Letters of introduction
11. Military related documents
12. Education
13. Prior travel
14. Occupation and work history
15. Financial information used to support visa application including bank statements, salary slips/letters, property records
16. Photos
17. Email addresses

5.20.4 Applications or Petitions for Immigration Benefits. USCIS may rcceive an application from an alien for immigration benefits or petitions. Depending on the completed form, USCIS may have information from the following non-exhaustive categories:

1.   Residences domestic and foreign
2.   Family Members (often extended family)
3.   Occupation
4.   Bank account information
5.   Biometrics
6.   Gender
7.   Identity documents
8.   Travel document information (and 1-94)
9.   Civil documents—POB, COC data
10. Employer/Prospective Employer
11. Religious Affiliations
12. Resumes
13. Educational Background
14. Past marriages or divorces
15. Biographical Information

5.20.5 ENCOUNTERS by HSPD-6 Foreign Partners. On some occasions, and based on the arrangement with and legal authorities of the particular foreign partner involved, an ENCOUNTER PACKAGE may include the KNOWN or SUSPECTED TERRORIST'S visa application to a foreign partner. One such student visa/permit application to a foreign partner could include information provided from the KNOWN or SUSPECTED TERRORIST in the following categories:

1.   Name as shown in passport
2.   Other names known by or ever known by
3.   Name in ethnic script
4.   Gender

5. Date of birth
6. Town/city of birth
7. Country of birth
8. Passport number, country, expiration date
9. Country of citizenship
10. Other citizenships held
11. Residential address and telephone number in home country
12. Local residential address and telephone number (if already in country)
13. Name and address for communication about this application
14. Name and address of friends, relatives, or contacts you have in the country (if applicable)
15. All periods of employment, including self-employment (to/from dates, name of employer, location, type of work/occupation/job title)
16. Financial information used to support visa application including bank statements, salary slips/letters, and property records
17. Length of planned stay in country
18. Questions concerning the person's character (e.g., whether the person has ever been convicted, charged, or under investigation for any offense(s) against the law in any country; ever deported, excluded or refused a visa by/removed from any country; and police certificates (as evidence of character) from home country or countries of citizenship and from all countries where the person has lived for five or more years since age 17)
19. Whether the application is for a student visa, a student permit, or a limited purpose visa
20. Whether the application is for a variation of conditions to work
21. Course of study and details of the course(s) enrolled
22. Arrangements for outward travel from host country
23. Name of legal guardian, other names legal guardian is known by, and relationship (e.g., mother, father, legal guardian)
24. Any national identity number or other unique identifier issued by a government
25. Any completed military service (e.g., from/to dates, rank, unit name or number, role)
26. Whether presently subject to military service obligation in any country
27. Any association with any intelligence agency or group, or law enforcement agency
28. Any association with any group or organization that has used or promoted violence to further their aims
29. Any involvement in war crimes, crimes against humanity, and/or human rights abuses
30. Payment method for application fee (e.g., bank check/draft, credit card, or personal check)

VIII. OBTAINING ENCOUNTER INFORMATION THROUGH TSC'S DAILY ENCOUNTER REPORTS

5.21 In addition to the aforementioned TSC/OI IIRs following an ENCOUNTER with a person who is a POSITIVE MATCH to a KNOWN or SUSPECTED TERRORIST, Agencies can obtain the Daily Summary Report (DSR) to assist them in identifying ENCOUNTERS of interest to their organizational missions. DSRs will contain as much information as legally permissible. DSRs are available from the following locations:

5.21.1 On the Secret Internet Protocol Router Network (SIPRNET), www.fbi.saov.aov/, click on the "TSC Intel Daily Summary Reports" link on the right side.

5.21.2 On Law Enforcement Online (LEO) via www.leo.gov

5.21.3 On Regional Information Sharing Systems via www.riss.net

5.21.4 On HS SLIC (for access contact state or local fusion center) or email: XXX@hq.dhs.gov

5.21.5 Two sources on FBINet:

      5.21.5.1 TSC's homepage at http://home.fbinet.lbi/nsb/tsc/Paaes/Default.aspx

      5.21.5.2 Current Intelligence Report at http://di.lbinet.fbi/ims/ciu/ciro/

Encounter	Situations	Encounter Packages		Notification of Encounter	Initial Review	Advanced Analysis	Target Analysis
Entity	Type	Data Format	Recipients	Responsible Entity	Encounter Information and new identificatiers entered into EMA	Responsible Entity	Responsible Entity
DMS/CBP/NTC	Apprehension Retention APIS Query ESTA Pre-Flight Inspection Land Border Crossing Vessel Manifest Carito Shipment night Manifests (Inbound and Outbound International)	Encounter Package	1. NCTC (posts to NOL, NOL-J. NOL-S) 2. FBI 3. DHS	1. TSOIJ-Operational Notification 2. TSC-OI (UR)-Community Notification	TSC/TSTOC (receives Electronic Referral)	FBI (Opens Cases, USPER, or KST is admitted/is in the US) DHS/I&A (is responsible for denied entries)	NCTC
DHS/ICE	Removal Investigation Extradition (in coordination with OOS and DO J) SEVIS Recurrent Vetting DHS National Security Overstay Initiative	Encounter Package	1. NCTC (posts to NOL. NOL-J. NOL-S) 2. FBI 3. DHS	1. TSOU-Operational Notification 2. TSC-OI (UR)-Community Notification	TSC/TSTOC (Reviews Electronic Referral)	FBI (Open coses. USPCR, or the KST Is odmltted/is in the U.S.) DHS/IAA (Is responsible for denied entries)	NCTC
DHS/TSA	Secure Flight Credentlallng (OIA) Pre-Flight Inspection Flight Manifests* Other	Encounter Package	1. NCTC (posts to NO!. NOL-J. NOL-S) 2. FBI 3. DHS	1. TSOU Operational Notification 2. TSC-OI (IIR¡-Community Notification	TSC/TSTOC (Reviews Electronic Referral)	FBI (Open coses. USPCR, or the KST Is odmltted/is in the U.S.) DHS/IAA (Is responsible for denied entries)	NCTC
DHS/USCIS	Applicant Petitioner Beneficiary	Application/ Previous Visa Applications	1. Ncrc (posts to NOL. NOL-J. NOL-S) 2. FBI 3. DHS 4. TSC	1. T SOU-Ope rational notification 2. TSC-OI (IIR¡-Community Notification	TSC/CIS (Reviews Application)	FBl (Open cases. USPCR. or the KST Is admitted/Is In the U.S.) DHS/IAA (Is responsible for denied entries)	NCTC
DHS/US Coast Guard	APIS Query Vessel Manifest Maritime Credentlallng Vessel & Port Inspections Investigations Lew Enforcement	Encounter Package	1. NCTC (posts to NO!. NOL-J. NOL-S) 2. FBI 3. DHS	1. TSOO Operational Notification 2. TSC-OI (IIR) Community Notification	TSC/TSTOC	FBI (Open cases. USPCR. or the KST Is admitted/Is in the U.S.) OHS/IS.A (1, responsible for denied entries)	NCTC
DHS/US Secret Service	investigations Political and Special Events	Encounter Package	1. NCTC (posts to NOL. NOL-J. NOL-S) 2. FBI 3. DHS	1. TSOU-Ope rational Notification 2. TSC-CM (IIR¡-Community	TSC/TSTOC	FBI (Open coses. USPCR. or the KST Is admitted/Is in the U.S.)	NCTC

				Notification			
DOS	Visa Application	Cur rent/ Prevlous Applications	1. NCTC (posts to NOL. NOL-J. NOL-S) 2. FBI 3. DOS 4. TSC	1. TSOU-Operational Notification 2. TSC-OI (IIR)- Community Notification	TSC/DOS (Reviews Visa Application)	NCTC FBI	NCTC
	Visa Revocations	Cur rent/ Prevlous Applications	1. NCTC (posts to NOL. NOL-J. NOL-S) 2. FBI 3. DOS 4. TSC	1. TSOU-Operational Notification 2. TSC-OI (IIR)- Community Notification	TSC/DOS (Reviews Visa Application)	NCTC FBI	NCTC
	Passport Application	Cur rent/ Prevlous Applications	1. NCTC (posts to NOL. NOL-J. NOL-S) 2. FBI 3. DOS 4. TSC	1. TSOU-Operational Notification 2. TSC-OI (IIR)- Community Notification	TSC/DOS (Reviews Visa Application)	NCTC FBI	NCTC
USAID	Benefits	Application (When Available	1. NCTC (post to NOL. NOL J. NOL S) 2. TSOu 3. TSC	1. TSOU-Operational Notification 2. TSC-OI (IIR)- Community Notification	TSC/USAID (Receives Electronic Referral)	NCTC	NCTC
Foreign Government	Remote Query International	Foreign Government POC Referral/ Application (When Available	1. NCTC (posts to NOL, NOL-J, NOL-S) 2. TSC	1. TSOU-Operational Notification 2. TSC-OI (IIR) Community Notification	TSC/TSTOC (Reviews Electronic Referral)	FBI (Open cases. USPCR. or the KST Is admitted/Is In the U.S.) NCTC	NCTC
	Legacy & Other Countries	Foreign Government POC Referral/ Application (When Available	1. NCTC (posts to NOL, NOL-J, NOL-S) 2. TSC	1. TSOU-Operational Notification 2. TSC-OI (IIR) Community Notification	TSC/DOS (Reviews Electronic Referral	FBI (Open cases. USPCR. or the KST Is admitted/Is In the U.S.) NCTC	NCTC
Law Enforcement	National Instant Background Checks / Traffic Violation / DoO Law Enforcement Investigation Jail Related Domestic Dispute Arrest Extradition	FBI CA/JTTF forwards Biometrics, Police Report (When Available	1. FBI 2. NCTC	1.TSOU Operational Notification 2. TSC-OI (IIR)- Community Notification	TSC/TSTOC (Via Telephone Call)	FBI (Open cases. USPCR. or the KST Is admitted/Is In the U.S.) NCTC	NCTC

•• Section II, Infra , Identifies categories of TERRORISM INFORMATION from encounters with positively identified KNOWN or SUSPECTED TERRORISTS that are of potential
Interest to NOMINATORS, other counterterrorism analysts, or the watchlisting community Encountering entitles should collect and share when it is within their legal authorities to retain and share TERRORISM INFORMATION.

Notes:

[82] Sharing information for reasons not related to KNOWN or SUSPECTED TERRORIST categories should be limited to updating biographic identifiers, and the sharing of relevant information that may assist in making decisions related to a change in a person's status in the TSDB and/or TERRORISM INFORMATION.

[83] Obligations include those imposed by IRTPA section 1021 or by interagency agreement (e.g., the

Information Sharing MOU (Appendix 5), the TSC MOU (Appendix 3) and Addendum B to the TSC MOU (Appendix 4)).

[84] CBP may also encounter such individuals in the course of processing an application and/or conducting an interview of an applicant for a trusted traveler program (e.g., NEXUS, Free and Secure Trade (FAST), Global Entry, SENTRI, etc.).

[85] For example, a U.S. PERSON who is a KNOWN or SUSPECTED TERRORIST may file a petition for a foreign national or a U.S. PERSON w h o is not a KNOWN or SUSPECTED TERRORIST may file a petition for a foreign national who is a KNOWN or SUSPECTED TERRORIST.

[86] Because USCIS is the custodian of information acquired through the immigration process relating to an individual and because the A-File is not routinely attached to the TSDB or TIDE, a specific request to USCIS is necessary in order to obtain information from the A-File.

[87] Consistent with section 428 of the Homeland Security Act and the Memorandum of Understanding between the Secretaries of Slate and Homeland Security Concerning Implementation of Section 428 of the Homeland Security Act of 2002, the Secretary o f Homeland Security may direct a consular officer to refuse or revoke a visa.

[88] See Appendix 3, TSC MOU.

[89] An "automated ingest" is one where the contents of TSC's EMA records are incorporated into NCTC's TIDE database via a system-to-system transfer of information that identifies new or changed information. This process allows NCTC to spot KNOWN or SUSPECTED TERRORIST records that have been amended or updated. This process also accommodates the transfer of attached ENCOUNTER PACKAGES received from SCREENERS. In those instances, the ENCOUNTER PACKAGES appear as attachments to the KNOWN or SUSPECTED TERRORIST record. ENCOUNTER PACKAGE attachments must be moved to another system in order to give the broader counterterrorism community access to the TERRORISM INFORMATION. That process is described in Section V, infra.

[90] Under governing authorities, the EBI can conduct "assessments" for an authorized purpose, such as obtaining information about a threat to national security, without a particular factual predication. T o open an investigation - whether a "preliminary" or " full" investigation - there must be a specific factual predication.

[91] See Paragraph 3(b) of the Information Sharing MOU (Appendix 5): "Reciprocity and Transparency. All information collected by any entity relevant to the missions and responsibilities of any other covered entities should be shared, to the greatest extent possible, between and among all covered entities. Likewise, the parties agree that, to the greatest extent possible, there should be transparency between and a m o n g the covered entities with regard to their activities to preempt, prevent, and disrupt TERRORIST attacks against U.S. PERSONS and interests. Except as otherwise specified in this Agreement, or mandated by relevant Federal statutes or Presidential Directives, procedures and mechanisms for information sharing, use, and handling shall be interpreted and implemented consistently and reciprocally regardless of the role a particular covered entity plays as a provider or recipient of covered information. In other words, for example, international TERRORISM INFORMATION collected by the Border Patrol should be shared by DHS with the IC to the same extent foreign intelligence information on TERRORISM is shared by the IC with DHS."

Appendix 1: DEFINITIONS

A. **ADVANCED ANALYSIS:** is a thorough review of the TERRORISM INFORMATION contained in an ENCOUNTER PACKAGE obtained as a result of the ENCOUNTER with the KNOWN or SUSPECTED TERRORIST. ADVANCED ANALYSIS includes the adding of TERRORIST IDENTIFIERS to existing KNOWN or SUSPECTED TERRORIST records and identifying new KNOWN or SUSPECTED TERRORISTS who should be nominated through the existing nomination process. In this context, ADVANCED ANALYSIS is being done on a tactical matter related to the specific KNOWN or SUSPECTED TERRORIST to identify information useful in "connecting the dots" between and among that KNOWN or SUSPECTED TERRORIST and other KNOWN or SUSPECTED TERRORISTS or potential KNOWN or SUSPECTED TERRORISTS. It is also when the need for foreign language translation services will be identified.

B.**AGGREGATORS:** are those who receive and hold TERRORISM INFORMATION and certain other non-TERRORlSM INFORMATION they are authorized to receive and retain.

C. **DEROGATORY INFORMATION:** is intelligence or information that demonstrates the nature of an individual's or group's association with TERRORISM and/or TERRORIST ACTIVITIES.

D. **ENCOUNTER:** is an event in which an individual is identified during a screening process to be a "POSITIVE MATCH," "POTENTIAL MATCH," or "INCONCLUSIVE MATCH," to an individual who has been designated in the TSDB as a KNOWN or SUSPECTED TERRORIST. An ENCOUNTER can be a face-to-face meeting with a KNOWN or SUSPECTED TERRORIST, electronic or a paper-based ENCOUNTER (e.g., the KNOWN or SUSPECTED TERRORIST has submitted an application for a benefit liked a visa, ETSA grant, or information is provided to the United States by a foreign government, aircraft operator, or other private entity).

E. **ENCOUNTERING AGENCY:** is a Department or Agency of the U.S. Government with TERRORIST screening or law enforcement responsibilities that comes into contact with a KNOWN or SUSPECTED TERRORIST (whether in a face-to-facc situation or via an electronic or written submission such as an application for a benefit) that the TSC determines is a POSITIVE MATCH to a KNOWN o r SUSPECTED TERRORIST.

F. **ENCOUNTER PACKAGE:** is all information gathered during an ENCOUNTER with a KNOWN or SUSPECTED TERRORIST.

G.
ENHANCEMENT: is the addition of new TERRORIST IDENTIFIERS or DEROGATORY INFORMATION on a KNOWN or SUSPECTED TERRORIST.

H. **FOREIGN FIGHTERS:** are nationals of one country who travel or attempt to travel to another country to participate in TERRORISM and/or TERRORIS T ACTIVITIES.

I. **FRAGMENTARY INFORMATION:** is information that suggests an individual may have a nexus to TERRORISM INFORMATION and/or TERRORIST ACTIVITIES but the information available to the NOMINATOR does not meet either or both the minimum identifying criteria that will facilitate identification of these individuals or the substantive DEROGATORY INFORMATION to meet the

REASONABLE SUSPICION standard but does qualify as information that should be provided to NCTC pursuant to HSPD-6.

J. **INCONCLUSIVE MATCH:** is the final determination by TSC that limited information in the subject data set matches TSDB data in a TSDB record and no additional identifiers are available to verify the match.

K. **INITIAL REVIEW:** is a quick primary review of the ENCOUNTER PACKAGE to identify obvious, new TERRORIST IDENTIFIERS about the KNOWN or SUSPECTED TERRORIST.

L. **KNOWN TERRORIST:** is an individual whom the U.S. Government knows is engaged, has been engaged, or who intends to engage in TERRORISM and/or TERRORIST ACTIVITY, including an individual (a) who has been, chargcd, arrested, indictcd, or convicted for a crime related to TERRORISM by U.S. Government or foreign government authorities; or (b) identified as a terrorist or member of a designated foreign terrorist organization pursuant to statute, Executive Order or international legal obligation pursuant to a United Nations Security Council Resolution.

M. **LONE WOLF:** an individual motivated by one or more extremists ideologies, who operates alone and supports, or engages in acts of violence in furtherance of that ideology or ideologies that may involve direction, assistance, or influence from a larger terrorist organization of a foreign actor.

N. **NOMINATOR or NOMINATING DEPARTMENT OR AGENCY:** is a Federal Department or Agency that has information to indicate that an individual meets the criteria for a KNOWN or SUSPECTED TERRORIST and nominates that individual to TIDE and the TSDB based on information that originated with that Department or Agcncy and/or a third Department or Agency.

O. **OPERATIONALLY CAPABLE:** as described in **Chapter 4**, an individual is "OPERATIONALLY CAPABLE" if, based on credible intelligence, he or she, acting individually or in concert with others, reasonably appears to have the ability, knowledge, opportunity, and intent or is actively seeking the opportunity to engage in a <u>violent</u> act of TERRORISM consistent with 18 U.S.C. 2331 or 18 U.S.C. 2332b. For example, attempting to obtain an IED would indicate an individual is OPERA TIONALLY CAPABLE of committing an act of TERRORISM. However, simply conducting internet research concerning lEDs would not be sufficient without additional activity. Depending on circumstances, and in combination with other facts, scouting potential targets or traveling for no legitimate purpose to places that have TERRORIST training grounds, regardless of whether the person is presently capable of using an IED, might also indicate an individual is OPERATIONALLY CAPABLE of committing an act of TERRORISM.

P. **ORIGINATOR:** is the Department or Agency that has appropriate subject matter interest and classification authority and collects TERRORISM INFORMATION (i.e., raw information) and disseminates it or TERRORIST IDENTIFIERS to other U.S. Government entities in an intelligence report (i.e., finished intelligence) or other mechanism.

Q. **PARTICULARIZED DEROGATORY INFORMATION:** is the type of information relied on to determine whether REASONABLE SUSPICION is met. This is information that demonstrates the nature of an individual's or group's association with TERRORISM and/or TERRORIST ACTIVITIES that is descriptive and specific to an event or activity, and is more than a label. For example, "Subject X provides false travel documentation for Al-Qaida operatives" is PARTICULARIZED DEROGATORY INFORMATION, whereas "Subject Y is a supporter," standing alone, is not considered

PARTICULARIZED DEROGATORY INFORMATION.

R. **POSITIVE MATCH:** occurs when the TSC determines that information about a subject encountered by a SCREENER exactly or reasonably matches a record in the TSDB.

S. **POTENTIAL MATCH:** occurs when an ENCOUNTERING AGENCY believes it has a match with a KNOWN or SUSPECTED TERRORIST record in the TSDB. An ENCOUNTERING AGENCY may attempt to resolve POTENTIAL MATCHES first through its review process. If an ENCOUNTERING AGENCY'S review process cannot resolve the individual's status as not a match to a TSDB record, the ENCOUNTERING AGENCY will refer the POTENTIAL MATCH to TSC for final adjudication.

T. **PURELY DOMESTIC TERRORISM INFORMATION:** is defined in the TSC MOU as information about U.S. PERSONS that has been determined to be PURELY DOMESTIC TERRORISM INFORMA TION with "no link to foreign intelligence, counterintelligence, or international TERRORISM."

U. **REASONABLE SUSPICION:** is the standard that must be met in order to include an individual in the TSDB, absent an exception provided for in the Watchlisting Guidance. To meet the REASONABLE SUSPICION standard, the NOMINATOR, based on the totality of the circumstances, must rely upon articulable intelligence or information which, taken together with rational inferences from those facts, reasonably warrants a determination that an individual is known or suspected to be or has been knowingly engaged in conduct constituting, in preparation for, in aid of, or related to TERRORISM and/or TERRORIST ACTIVITIES. There must be an objective factual basis for the NOMINATOR to believe that the individual is a KNOWN or SUSPECTED TERRORIST. Mere guesses or hunches are not enough to constitute a REASONABLE SUSPICION that an individual is a KNOWN or SUSPECTED TERRORIS T. Reporting of suspicious activity alone that does not meet the REASONABLE SUSPICION standard set forth herein is not a sufficient basis to watchlist an individual. The facts, however, given fair consideration, should sensibly lead to the conclusion that an individual is, or has, engaged in TERRORISM and/or TERRORIST ACTIVITIES.

V. **SCREENER:** a Department or Agency that is authorized to conduct TERRORISM screening to determine if an individual is a possible match to a KNOWN or SUSPECTED TERRORIST in the TSDB. SCREENERS can include Federal Departments or Agencies, state, local, tribal, territorial, or foreign governments and certain private entities. The term 'SCREENER' is used throughout this document as a general reference to a government official who compares an individual's information with information in the TSDB to determine if an individual is in the TSDB. Law enforcement officials who engage in such activities may normally describe their targeting or other actions in this context as other than "screening." For ease of reference, government officials who compare an individual's information with information in the TSDB will be referred to in the Watchlisting Guidance as a "SCREENER."

W. **SUSPECTED TERRORIST:** is an individual who is REASONABLY SUSPECTED to be, or has been engaged in conduct constituting, in preparation for, in aid of, or related to TERRORISM and/or TERRORIST ACTIVITIES based on an articulable and REASONABLE SUSPICION.

X. **TARGETED ANALYSIS:** is further exploitation of a targeted set of ENCOUNTER PACKAGES and ADVANCED ANALYSIS products to assist in identifying TERRORIST trends and changes to methods, tactics, and practices. ENCOUNTERS for TARGETED ANALYSIS are selected using contemporaneous threat criteria, and research in additional repositories. Contemporaneous threat criteria include association with a priority terrorist group (e.g., NIPF Tier I or II); ENCOUNTERS with KNOWN or SUSPECTED TERRORISTS designated as No Fly or associated with violent activity; or at the request of any Department or Agency that identifies a need.

Y. **TERRORISM AND/OR TERRORIST ACTIVITIES:** is a combination of definitions because none of the federal law definitions of "terrorism" or "terrorist activities" were directly applicable to the consolidated approach to watchlisting. For terrorist watchlisting purposes under this Watchlisting Guidance, "terrorism and/or terrorist activities" combine elements from various federal definitions and are considered to: (a) involve violent acts or acts dangerous to human life, property, or infrastructure that may be a violation of U.S. law, or may have been, if those acts were committed in the United States; and, (b) appear intended to intimidate or cocrcc a civilian population, influence the policy of a government by intimidation or coercion, or affect the conduct of government by mass destruction, assassination, kidnapping, or hostage-taking. This includes activities that facilitate or support TERRORISM and/or TERRORIST ACTIVITIES, such as providing a safe house, transportation, communications, funds, transfer of funds or other material benefit, false documentation or identification, weapons (including chemical, biological, or radiological weapons), explosives, or training for the commission of act of terrorism and/or TERRORIST ACTIVITY.

Z. **TERRORISM INFORMATION:** applies, where appropriate, to purely domestic terrorism as defined in the TSC MOU and incorporates the definition found in in section 1016 of the IRTPA (6 U.S.C. 485), as amended. The term "TERRORISM INFORMATION" means -

1. all information, whether collected, produced, or distributed by intelligence, law enforcement, military, homeland security, or other activities relating to—
   a) the existence, organization, capabilities, plans, intentions, vulnerabilities, means of finance or material support, or activities of foreign or international terrorist groups or individuals, or of domestic groups or individuals involved in transnational TERRORISM;
   b) threats posed by such groups or individuals to the United States, U.S. PERSONS, or United States interests, or to those of other nations;
   c) communications of or by such groups or individuals; or
   d) groups or individuals reasonably believed to be assisting or associated with such groups or individuals; and
2. includes weapons of mass destruction information.
   a) Weapons of Mass Destruction Information: information that could reasonably be expected to assist in the development, proliferation, or use of a weapon of mass destruction (including a chemical, biological, radiological, or nuclear weapon) that could be used by a TERRORIST or a terrorist organization against the United States, including information about the location of any stockpile of nuclear materials that could be exploited for use in such a weapon that could be used by a TERRORIST or a terrorist organization against the United States.

AA. **TERRORISM SCREENING INFORMATION:** is defined in the standard HSPD-6 agreement to mean unclassified identifying information about KNOWN or SUSPECTED TERRORISTS.

BB. **TERRORIST:** please see KNOWN TERRORIST or SUSPECTED TERRORIST.

CC. **TERRORIST IDENTIFIERS:** are referred to in the TSC MOU as U//FOUO data for inclusion into the TSDB. TERRORIST IDENTIFIERS are data points about a particular identity that include names and aliases, dates of birth, places of birth, unique identifying numbers, passport information, country of origin and nationality, physical identifiers, addresses, photographs or renderings of the individual, fingerprints or other biomctric data, employment data, license plate numbers, and any other TERRORISM INFORMATION that ORIGINA TORS specifically provide for passage to the TSC.

DD. **TERRORIST INFORMATION:** as defined in HSPD-6 is "information about individuals known or appropriately suspected to be or have been engaged in conduct constituting, in preparation for, in aid of, or related to TERRORISM."

EE. **U.S. PERSON:** is defined in Executive Order 12333 (as amended) as "a United States citizen, an alien known by the intelligence element concerned to be a permanent resident alien, an unincorporated association substantially composed of United States citizens or permanent resident aliens, or a corporation incorporated in the United States, except for a corporation directed and controlled by a foreign government or governments." The Watchlisting Guidance contains certain exceptions to the minimum substantive derogatory standards for TERRORIST watchlisting that support immigration and visa screening activities by the DHS and DOS to determine whether ineligibilities exist for admission to the United States or visa adjudication pursuant to the 1NA. Because the 1NA defines "aliens" as any person not a citizen or national of the United States, the INA admissibility provisions also apply to LPRs, in certain circumstances, who are considered as U.S. PERSONS under Executive Order 12333. Consequently, NCTC developed a mechanism in TIDE to identify and distinguish U.S. citizens from non-U.S. citizens in order to further distinguish between "aliens" under the INA and U.S. PERSONS under Executive Order 12333. See INA § 101(a)(3) [8 U.S.C. 1101(a)(3)],

Appendix 2: Homeland Security Presidential Directive/HSPD-6

For Immediate Release
Office of the Press Secretary
September 16. 2003

Homeland Security Presidential Directive/Hspd-6

Subject. Integration and Use of Screening Information

To protect against terorism it is the policy of the United States to (1) develop, integrate, and maintain thorough, accurate, and current information about individuals known or appropriately suspected to be or have been engaged in conduct constituting, in preparation for, in aid of. or related to terrorism (Terrorist Information), and (2) use that information as appropriate and to the full extent permitted by law to support (a) Federal. State. local, territorial, tribal, foreign-government, and private-sector screening processes, and (b) diplomatic, military, intelligence, law enforcement, immigration, visa, and protective processes

This directive shall be implemented in a manner consistent with the provisions of the Constitution and applicable laws, including those protecting the rights of all Americans.

To further strengthen the ability of the United States Government to protect the people, property, and territory of fhe United States against acts of terrorism, and to the full extent permitted by law and consistent with the policy set forth above:

(1) The Attorney General shall establish an organization to consolidate the Government's approach to terrorism screening and provide for the appropriate and lawful use of Terrorist Information in screening processes

(2) The heads of executive departments and agencies shall, to the extent permitted by law. provide to the Terrorist Threat Integration Center (TTIC) on an ongoing basis all appropriate Terrorist Information in their possession, custody, or control The Attorney General, in coordination with the Secretary of State, the Secretary of Homeland Security, and the Director of Central Intelligence shall implement appropriate procedures and safeguards with respect to all such information about United States persons. The TTIC will provide the organization referenced in paragraph (1) with access to all appropriate information or intelligence in the TTIC's custody, possession, or control that the organization requires to perform its functions.

(3) The heads of executive departments and agencies shall conduct screening using such information at all appropriate opportunities, and shall report to the Attorney General not later than 90 days from the date of this directive, as to the opportunities at which such screening shall and shall not be conducted

(4) The Secretary of Homeland Security shall develop guidelines to govern the use of such information to support State, local, territorial, and tribal screening processes, and private sector screening processes that have a substantial bearing on homeland security.

(5) The Secretary of State shall develop a proposal for my approval for enhancing cooperation with

certain foreign governments, beginning with those countries for which the United States has waived visa requirements, to establish appropriate access to terrorism screening information of the participating governments

This directive does not alter existing authorities or responsibilities of department and agency heads to carry out operational activities or provide or receive information This directive is intended only to improve the internal management of the executive branch and is not intended to, and does not, create any right or benefit enforceable at law or in equity by any party against the United States, its departments, agencies, entities, officers, emoloyees or agents, or any other person

The Attorney General, in consultation with the Secretary of State, the Secretary of Homeland Security, and the Director of Central Intelligence, shall report to me through the Assistant to the President for Homeland Security not later than October 31. 2003. on progress made to implement this directive and shall thereafter repor. to me on such progress or any recommended changes from time to time as appropriate.

GEORGE W BUSH

###

Appendix 3: TSC MOU

THE SECRETARY OF STATE
THE ATTORNEY GENERAL
THE SECRETARY OF HOMELAND SECURITY
THE DIRECTOR OF CENTRAL INTELLIGENCE

MEMORANDUM OF UNDERSTANDING
ON THE INTEGRATION AND USE OF SCREENING INFORMATION
TO PROTECT AGAINST TERRORISM

(1) This memorandum represents the consensus view of the Secretary of State, the Attorney General, the Secretary of Homeland Security, and the Director of Central Intelligence-regarding the implementation of Homeland Security Presidential Directive-6 (HSPD-6), dated September 16. 2003, entitled "Integration and Use of Screening Information to Protect Against Terrorism."

(2) Consistent with the President's direction, the Parties to this Memorandum will develop and maintain, to the extent permitted by law, the most thorough, accurate, and current information possible about individuals known or appropriately suspected to be or have been involved in activities constituting, in preparation for, in aid of, or related to terrorism ("Terrorist Information"), and will, as described in this Memorandum:

(a) use that information to support screening processes at all appropriate opportunities;

(b) make accessible appropriate information to State, local, territorial, and tribal authorities to support their screening processes and otherwise enable them to identify, or assist in identifying, such individuals;

(c) host mechanisms, to the extent permitted by law, to support appropriate private sector screening processes that have a substantial bearing on homeland security;

(d) host mechanisms, to the extent permitted by law, to support appropriate foreign government screening processes that have a substantial bearing on homeland security;

(e) provide or make accessible appropriate information to foreign governments cooperating with the United States in the war on terrorists of global reach; and

(f) ensure that these activities are carried out in a manner consistent with the Constitution and applicable laws.

Terrorist Screening Center

(3) To implement the President's directive, the Attorney General, acting through the Director of the FBI, and in coordination with the Secretary of State, the Secretary of Homeland Security, and the Director of Central Intelligence, will establish the Terrorist Screening Center to consolidate the

Government's approach to terrorism screening and provide for the appropriate and lawful use of Terrorist Information, in screening processes.

(4) The Terrorist Screening Center will:

(a) maintain a consolidated terrorist screening database that is a continuously updated, sensitive but unclassified subset of the Terrorist Information possessed by the TTIC, and the Purely Domestic Terrorism Information (i.e., information about U.S. persons that has been determined to be purely domestic terrorism information with no link to foreign intelligence, counterintelligence, or international terrorism) possessed by the FBI;

(b) determine, for each entry in the consolidated tenorist screening database, which supported screening processes shall query that entry, as described in paragraphs (15) through (24);

(c) ensure, consistent with applicable law, that appropriate information possessed by State, local, territorial, and tribal governments, which is available to the Federal government, is considered in determinations made by the Terrorist Screening Center;

(d) host mechanisms to support appropriate screening processes; and

(e) provide continual operational support to assist in the identification of persons screened and, when an individual known or appropriately suspected to be involved in activities constituting, in preparation for, in aid of, or related to terrorism, has been identified through a screening process, facilitate, to the extent permitted by law, appropriate and lawful actions to be taken by appropriate departments and agencies.

(5) The Terrorist Screening Center will be headed by a senior U.S. Government official (the Director of the Terrorist Screening Center), who will report to the Attorney General through the Director of the FBI. The Director of the Terrorist Screening Center will be appointed by the Attorney General, in consultation with the Secretary of Homeland Security, the Secretary of State, the Director of the FBI, and the Director of Central Intelligence. The Principal Deputy Director of the Terrorist Screening Center will be a senior official from the Department of Homeland Security.

(6) The Terror,st Screening Center will be staffed with assignees and other officials from the Department of State, the Department of Justice, the Department of Homeland Security, and other Federal departments and agencies that the Terrorist Screening Center supports. The Director of Central Intelligence, acting in his capacity as statutory head of the Intelligence Community, may also determine that assignees of other appropriate agencies, within the Intelligence Community, will be made available to perform appropriate duties at the Terrorist Screening Center.

(7) Personnel assigned to the Terrorist Screening Center will have appropriate access to the TTIC database and any relevant intelligence information necessary to perform the Terrorist Screening Center's functions. To the extent required by law, the Parties to this Memorandum may jointly determine the circumstances under which personnel from the Intelligence Community, assigned to the Terrorist Screening Center in accordance with paragraph (6), may participate in the functions of the Terrorist Screening Center relating to U.S. persons.

(8) The Director of the Terrorist Screening Center will establish necessary procedures and safeguards to ensure the Terrorist Screening Center's functions are canied out in a manner consistent with the

Constitution and applicable laws, including, but not limited to, procedures to:

(a) address the repeated misidentification of persons in any U.S. Government screening process;

(b) regularly review information, and to promptly adjust or delete erroneous or outdated information; and

(c) protect personal privacy.

(9) Consistent with the President's directive, the Secretary of State, in consultation with the Secretary of Homeland Security, the Attorney General, and the Director of Central Intelligence, and working with the Director of the Terrorist Screening Center, not later than 180 days from today, will recommend to the President through the Assistant to the President for Homeland Security and the Assistant to the President for National Security Affairs, a proposal for cooperating with certain foreign governments (beginning with those countries for which the United States has waived visa requirements) to establish appropriate access to terrorist screening information of the participating governments, in a manner consistent with each government's laws, and to provide operational support to the participating governments.

Terrorist Threat Integration Center (TTIC) Identities Database

(10) The TTIC database will include, to the extent permitted by law, all information the U.S. government possesses related to the identities of individuals known or appropriately suspected to be or have been involved in activities constituting, in preparation for, in aid of, or related to terrorism, with the exception of Purely Domestic Terrorism Information.

(11) As directed by the President, and to the extent permitted by law, Federal departments and agencies will provide to the TTIC on an ongoing basis all relevant Terrorist Information in their possession, custody, or control, with the exception of Purely Domestic Terrorism Information, which will instead be provided directly to the FBI. Departments and agencies will continue to provide new or updated information, and adjust or retract information as needed, in as near to real-time as possible. To this end, the Parties to this Memorandum will automate, to the maximum extent possible while providing for necessary review, their processes and mechanisms for securely sharing this information, including, but not limited to, the following:

(a) The Secretary of State, the Attorney General, the Secretary of Homeland Security, and the Director of Central Intelligence, in coordination with other relevant department and agency heads, not later than 180 days from today, will jointly recommend to the President through the Assistant to the President for Homeland Security, in consultation with the Assistant to the President for National Security Affairs, improvements, if any, to the existing cable-based system of sharing terrorism-related information with other departments and agencies.

(b) The Attorney General will ensure that the FBI's information technology modernization programs incorporate automated means of sharing appropriate information with the TT1C and other departments and agencies, while providing for necessary review, in near real-time.

(12) The TTIC identities database, and the FBI's database containing Purely Domestic Terrorism

Information, will incorporate, to the extent permitted by law, available biometric data, including data on persons who even if otherwise unidentified are known or appropriately suspected to be or have been involved in activities constituting, in preparation for, in aid of, or related to terrorism. The databases will have the capability of periodically incorporating advancements in biometric technology.

Relationship of the TTIC and FBI Databases to the Terrorist Screening Center Terrorist Screening Database

(13) The TTIC identities database will serve, with the exception described in paragraph (10), as the single source for the Terrorist Screening Center terrorist screening database. The Director of the FBI will serve as the source for the Terrorist Screening Center terrorist screening database with regard to Purely Domestic Terrorism Information. The Terrorist Screening Center terrorist screening database will be a continuously updated, sensitive but unclassified subset of the Terrorist Information possessed by the TTIC, and the Purely Domestic Terrorism Information possessed by the FBI.

Terrorist Screening Center Terrorist Screening Database

(14) The Director of the TTIC, the Director of the Terrorist Screening Center, and the heads of Federal departments and agencies, or their designees, may nominate persons for inclusion in the terrorist screening database, with notification, as appropriate, to the Director of the TTIC and/or the Director of the FBI.

(15) The Terrorist Screening Center will determine, according to criteria established jointly with the entity responsible for each supported screening proccss, which supported screening processes will query that entry in the consolidated terrorist screening database. The Terrorist Screening Center will make these determinations based on criteria and procedures developed in coordination with the Parties to this Memorandum and in consultation with the heads of appropriate Federal departments and agencies, based on faclors including, but not limited to, the following:

(a) the nature of the person's association with terrorism;

(b) the quality of the data, including credibility, reliability, and extent of corroboration;

(c) the extent cf uniquely identifying data;

(d) the authority or authorities under which the data was obtained, and any restrictions on how it may be shared or used;

(e) the authority or authorities of the screening entity;

(f) the circumstances, including changes in the Homeland Security Alert Level, under which screening will occur; and

(g) the action the screening entity will take if a person is identified as a person in the terrorist screening database.

(16) The Director of the Terrorist Screening Center, in coordination with the Parties to this Memorandum and in consultation with the heads of appropriate Federal departments and agencies, will establish procedures to review the continued inclusion of a person in the terrorist screening database, and to review the inclusion of that person in particular screening processes as described in paragraph (15) above, whenever new information about that person is developed.

(17) Except upon written direction from the President, determinations to include U.S. persons in the terrorist screening database based solely on information concerning the domestic activities of such persons will be made as appropriate by the Secretary of State, the Attorney General, and the Secretary of Homeland Security, or their designees.

(18) The Attorney General, acting through the Director of the Terrorist Screening Center, will review each nomination and determine whether to include that person in those records that can be queried by law enforcement authorities through the NCIC database; for aliens, the Attorney General will do so in consultation with the Secretary of Homeland Security, acting through the Secretary of Homeland Security's representative assigned to the Terrorist Screening Center.

(19) The Secretary of Homeland Security, acting through his representative assigned to the Terrorist Screening Center, will review each nomination and determine whether to include that person in those records that can be queried by, or made accessible by appropriate means, to other State, local, territorial, and tribal officials for homeland security purposes, including, but not limited to, screening persons when they apply for driver's licenses or other forms of identification.

(20) The Secretary of Homeland Security, acting through his representative assigned to the Terrorist Screening Center, will review each nomination and determine whether to include that person in those records that will be subject to queries submitted by appropriate private sector critical infrastructure operators or organizers of large events. The Secretary of Homeland Security, in consultation with the other Parties to this Memorandum, and working with the Director of the Terrorist Screening Center, will establish necessary guidelines and criteria to:

(a) govern the mechanisms by which private sector entities can submit such queries; and

(b) initiate appropriate law enforcement or other governmental action, if any, when a person submitted for query by a private sector entity is identified as a person in the terrorist screening database.

(21) The Secretary of State in consultation with the Attorney General, the Secretary of Homeland Security, and the Director of Central Intelligence, acting through their representatives assigned to the Terrorist Screening Center, will review each nomination and determine whether to include that person ir. those records that can be queried by, or made accessible by appropriate means to, foreign governments cooperating with the United States in the war on terrorists of global reach.

[Paragraphs (22) - (24) are classified and therefore redacted]

(25) The terrorist screening database will be accessible to screening processes on a real-time basis. Screening processes will only be able to access those records that have been identified and approved for such screening, as described in paragraphs (15) through (24) above. The Director of the Terrorist Screening Center will strictly limit, to the maximum extent possible, the need to provide U.S. Government terrorist screening data in list form to supported entities.

Additional Implementation Provisions

(26) Per the President's direction, and consistent with guidelines developed by the Attorney General in coordination with the other Parlies to this Memorandum, the heads of Federal departments and agencies will conduct screening using the Terrorist Screening Center database at all appropriate opportunities, and shall report to the Attorney General not later than 90 days from today the screening opportunities at which such screening shall and shall not be conducted.

(27) The Attorney General and the Secretary of Homeland Security will conduct a review of the organization, structure and progress of the Terrorist Screening Center at an appropriate time, and report to the President through the Assistant to the President for Homeland Security. The report will include a recommendation on whether any modifications to the Terrorist Screening Center should be made.

(28) To the extent permitted by law, the Director of the TTIC will promptly assume responsibility for the functions and personnel of the Department of State's TTPOFF counterteriorist program, less those components devoted to providing operational support to TIPOFF users and will ensure that all terrorist identity information contained within the TIPOFF database is fully integrated into the TTIC database. The functionality of the TIPOFF program, whereby consular officials receive near real-time feedback to hits to TIPOFF entries, will be maintained or improved upon. A seperate Annex to this Memorandum will be promptly agreed to regarding the modalities of TIPOFF relocation to the TTIC, and the specific responsibilities of each party.

(29) Beginning with the standup of the Terrorist Screening Center, Federal departments and agencies will discontinue or transfer to the Terrorist Screening Center, to the extent permitted by law and with appropriate consultation with the Congress, those operations that are duplicative of the Terrorist Screening Center's mission to provide continuous operational support to users of the terrorist screening database, including but not limited to:

(a) those components of the Department of State's TIPOFF counterterrorist program devoted to providing operational support to TIPOFF users (with the exception of a small element that will remain at the Department of State to facilitate intelligence support to the Bureau of Consular Affairs);

(b) the FBI's Watchlist Unit; and

(c) the Transportation Security Agency's No-Fly and Selectee list program.

(30) Consistent with HSPD-6 and other presidential directives, this Memorandum does not alter existing authorities or responsibilities of the heads of Federal departments and agencies to carry out operational activities or provide or receive information.

(31) To the extent that existing notices are not sufficient, the Parties to this Memorandum, which will provide information to the TTIC, the FBI, and/or the Terrorist Screening Center under HSPD-6 and this Memorandum, will publish in the Federal Register, prior to the standup of the Terrorist Screening Center, "routine use" notices under the Privacy Act sufficient to indicate that such information will be provided.

(32) This Memorandum of Understanding is effective from the date of signature by all Parties. Any Party may submit, through the Assistant to the President for Homeland Security, written requests for revisions, amendments, modifications, annexes and supplemental understanding to this Memorandum at any time. Such changes shall become effective upon the date of approval by ail Parties. The Parties shall review this Memorandum not later than one year from its effective date.

Colin L Powell
Secretary of State

John Ashcroft
Attorney General

Thomas J Ridge
Secretary of Homeland Security

George J. Tenet
Director of Central Intelligence

Signatures are consolidated from classified version of the original TSC MOU.

APPENDIX 4: ADDENDUM B TO TSC MOU

THE SECRETARY OF STATE
THE SECRETARY OF THE TREASURY
THE SECRETARY OF DEFENSE
THE ATTORNEY GENERAL
THE SECRETARY OF HOMELAND SECURITY
THE DIRECTOR OF NATIONAL INTELLIGENCE
THE DIRECTOR OF THE CENTRAL INTELLIGENCE AGENCY
THE DIRECTOR OF THE NATIONAL COUNTERTERRORISM CENTER
THE DIRECTOR OF THE TERRORIST SCREENING CENTER

ADDENDUM B

TO THE
MEMORANDUM OF UNDERSTANDING ON THE INTEGRATION AND USE OF
SCREENING INFORMATION TO PROTECT AGAINST TERRORISM

Background

(1) This Addendum, ("Addendum B") supplements the Memorandum of Understanding on the Integration and Use of Screening Information to Protect Against Terrorism, dated September 16, 2003, ("the TSC MOU") and supercedes Addendum A, effective August 2, 2004. To the extent that Addendum B is inconsistent with the TSC MOU, Addendum B supercedes the TSC MOU. In addition, Addendum B supercedes the TIPOFF-TERROR Memorandum of Understanding, dated June 4, 2002. between the Department of State, the Defease Intelligence Agency, the National Security Agency. the Federal Bureau of Investigation, and the Central Intelligence Agency or any other interim agreement intended to address the use of disseminated Terrorism Information.

(2) Addendum B incorporates by reference all provisions of the Memorandum of Understanding between, the Intelligence Community, Federal Law Enforcement Agencies, and the Department of Homeland Security Concerning information Sharing, dated March 4, 2003 (the Information Sharing MOU") and the TSC MOU. By their signatures on Addendum A, the Secretary of State, the Secretary of the Treasury, and the Secretary of Defense became signatories of the Information Sharing MOU and the TSC MOU and agree that all provisions of those MOUs apply to all entities that are, or become, wholly or in part, part of, respectively, the Department of State, the Department of the Treasury and the Department of Defense. To the extent that the TSC MOU and Addendum B provide for greater information sharing than that mandated by the Information Sharing MOU, the provisions of the TSC MOU and Addendum B shall control the Parties' actions. In all other respects, to the extent that provisions of the TSC MOU and/or Addendum B are inconsistent with the Information Sharing MOU,

the provisions of the Information Sharing MOU shall control the actions of the Parties to this Addendum.

Purpose

(3) The purposes of Addendum B are:

(a) to ensure the full implementation of subparagraph (2) of Homeland Security Presidential Directive-6 (HSPD-6), dated September 16, 2003, entitled "Integration and Use of Screening Information to Protect Against Terrorism:" and

(b) to memorialize the Parties' agreement that they will, to the maximum extent permitted by law and consistent with the President's direction for the establishment of the Terrorist Threat Integration Center, now the National Counterterrorism Center (NCTC) and the Information Sharing MOU, provide to the NCTC on an ongoing basis all Terrorism Information (as defined is the Intelligence Reform and Terrorism Prevention Act (IRTPA) of 2004, Section 1016(a)(4)) in their possession, custody, or control.

Procedures

(4) The Parties will, to the maximum extent permitted by law and consistent with the establishment of the NCTC, the Information Sharing MOU. and in furtherance of the information sharing mandates in IRTPA, provide to the NCTC, on an ongoing basis, all Terrorism Information, in their possession, custody, or control If additional procedures and mechanisms are needed beyond those directed in the Information Sharing MOU and IRTPA to accomplish this including, but not limited to. compartmented programs, the NCTC, in coordination with the Parties disseminating the Terrorism Information ("Originators'), shall establish procedures to guide the provision of such information, and the Parties shall establish procedures and mechanisms to provide such information.

(5) A web-based version of the NCTC Identities Database, the Terrorist Identities Datamart Environment (TIDE-Ordine), as mandated in the TSC MOU, will be available to all individuals who have obtained an IC certificate for access to NCTC Online (NOL), formerly known as CTLINK, which is a Community of Interest on INTELINK. The NCTC will make available to the Parties upon request, the names and clearances of personnel with access to TIDE-Online. All users will be responsible for complying with the conditions set for access to TIDE-Online.

(6) When the Parties provide disseminated Terrorism Information to the NCTC, no specific notification will occur between the NCTC and the Originator identifying the fact that Terrorism Information contained in those communications were placed in TIDE.

(7) The Parties authorize the NCTC (and the FBI for Purely Domestic Terrorism Information, as defined in the TSC MOU) to provide to the TSC the following data (referred to as, "Terrorist Identifiers"), in accordance with tbe provisions of paragraph (8) below, for inclusion in the TSCs consolidated terrorist screening database (TSDB):

    (a) Names and aliases;
    (b) Dates of birth;

(c) Places of birth;

(d) Unique identifying numbers such as alien registration numbers, visa numbers, social security account numbers;

(e) Passport information, including passport numbers, countries of issuance, dates and locations of issuance, expiration dates, passport photos, and other relevant data;

(f) Countries of origin and nationalities;

(g) Physical identifiers, such as sex, race, height, weight, eye color, hair color, scars, marks, or tattoos;

(h) Known locations, i.e. addresses;

(i) Photographs or renderings of the individual;

(j) Fingerprints or other biometric data;

(k) Employment data;

(l) License plate numbers;

(m) Any other Terrorism Information that Originators specifically provide for passage to the TSC.

(8) Once provided to the NCTC (or the FBI for Purely Domestic Terrorism Information), the Parties agree that the NCTC (or the FBI for Purely Domestic Terrorism Information) will deem the Terrorist Identifies listed in paragraph (7) For Official Use Only (FOUO) for the purposes of providing the data to the TSC for Inclusion in TSDB. These Terrorist Identifiers passed to the TSC and retained in TSDB will be deemed FOUO.

(9) The Originator may prohibit the NCTC from passing the Terrorist Identifier(s) identified in (a) - (m) above to the TSC as FOUO data for inclusion in TSDB if an appropriate official so authorizes. Each Originator shall identify its Terrorist Identifier(s) that are to be prohibited from being passed to the TSC for inclusion in TSDB by marking those items, "TIDE restricted." Restrictions on use shall be imposed only to the extent strictly necessary to prevent the unauthorized disclosure of information that clearly identifies, or would reasonably permit ready identification of intelligence or sensitive law enforcement sources, methods, activities or cryptology that are particularly susceptible to countermeasures that would nullify or measurably reduce their effectiveness.

(10) The Parties agree that subject to an Originator's ability to prohibit specific Terrorist Identifiers from being included in TSDB, all Terrorist Identifiers listed in (7) may be passed to the TSC, regardless of the date or classification of tha disseminated Terrorism Information.

(11) Nothing in Addendum B shall inhibit or delay the provision of Terrorism Information to the NCTC.

(12) Absent prior approval by the Originator, information (including all information designated classified or FOUO in TIDE and information in TSDB) may not be used in any legal or administrative proceeding or process, including any judicial or quasi-judicial process, presentation to grand or petit juries, submission as part of an application for subpoenas, orders for electronic surveillance, search or arrest warrants, presentation as evidence, or any use that could result in public disclosure. Information from FISA collection, or derived, therefrom may only be used in legal or administrative proceeding or process with the advance authorization of the Attorney General. Any recipient of information from TSDB interested in obtaining authorization to use that information in a legal or administrative proceeding or process must contact the TSC to obtain the approval of the Originator. If TSDB information is from FISA collection, or derived therefrom, the TSC through FBI Headquarters, will obtain the necessary Attorney General authorization. Any reproduction, dissemination, or

communication (including, but not limited to, oral briefings) of any information from TSDB must be accompanied by a statement of these restrictions. Nothing in this paragraph shall inhibit the sharing of a limited set of Terrorist Identifiers: name; date of birth; passport number; passport country of origin/citizenship, with state, local and tribal authorities, or foreign governments for terrorism screening purposes, as permitted by law, regulation, or agreement of the Parties.

(13) When an individual in TSDB has been positively identified during a screening encounter, the Parties will provide the NCTC with Terrorism Information collected during the encounter, such as photographs, fingerprints, copies of pocket liner, copies of written data, any reports of Terrorism Information provided by that individual, or other items of potential interest, for inclusion in TIDE. The NCTC and/or the TSC will, in partnership with departments and agencies which are not Parties to Addendum B, but which conduct screening using TSDB, establish procedures to ensure that, when an individual in TSDB has been positively identified during a screening encounter, those departments and agencies will provide the NCTC and all appropriate agencies that have a counterterrorism mission, with Terrorism Information as described above.

(14) The Director of the TSC shall establish procedural safeguards, including, but not limited to, training, standard operating procedures, and caller authentication procedures, and implement technological safeguards, including, but not limited to, the use of firewalls and public key encryption, to minimize the unauthorised disclosure of information, and to reduce the vulnerability of TSDB to unauthorised access or exploitation. The establishment of these safeguards shall in no way inhibit or delay the provision of information to the NCTC or the TSC.

(15) Addendum B amends Director of Central Intelligence Directive 2/4 (DCID 2/4) by replacing the term "Terrorist threat-related information," wherever it appears in DCID2/4, with the term Terrorism information, as defined in the IRTPA.

Implementation

(16) Addendum B is effective from the date of signature by all Parties and applies to all disseminated Terrorism Information, regardless of the date of the document in which it is contained. Addendum B may be signed in counterparts.

(17) The NCTC, the TSC, and the Parties, in coordination with appropriate Originators, shall report to the Homeland Security Advisor from time to time as appropriate, on the progress made to implement Addendum B.

(18) Nothing in Addendum B alters, or impedes the ability or authority of federal departments and agencies to perform their responsibilities under law, consistent with applicable legal authorities and Presidential guidance. Specifically, nothing in Addendum B alters the information sharing requirements of the Homeland Security Act or the requirements of the IRTPA.

SIGNED
Secretary of State   Attorney General
Secretary of the Treasury   Secretary of Homeland Security
Secretary of Defense   Director of National Intelligence

Director, Central Intelligence Agency   Director, Terrorism Screening Center
Director, National Counterterrorism Center

APPENDIX 5: INFORMATION SHARING MOU

THE DIRECTOR OF CENTRAL INTELLIGENCE
WASHINGTON, DC 20505

DAC-51355-03
4 March 2003

MEMORANDUM FOR: National Foreign Intelligence Program Principals

SUBJECT: Homeland Security Information Sharing Memorandum of Understanding

1. The Attorney General, Secretary of Homeland Security, and I have just signed the attached Memorandum of Understanding on Information Sharing (MOU) implementing information sharing requirements of the Homeland Security Act (Act) . It is effective immediately. As you know, the Department of Homeland Security (Department) has now reached critical mass. Our corresponding intelligence support function, has also matured.

2. As with much recent homeland security-related work, the drafting process on this high priority White House initiative moved quickly. successive drafts were sent to each of your agencies, with all comments forwarded directly to the White House drafting team. The resulting MOU is a fair expression of what the Act requires. I expect each of you to hold those you supervise accountable for giving full effect to each of the MOU's provisions. Note that the MOU makes Associate Director of Central Intelligence for Homeland Security. Winston P. Wiley my representative for information sharing under the MOU. He has my proxy and full support.

3. Full and efficient implementation of the MOU will benefit not only the Department, but also intelligence and law enforcement agencies. As with the Terrorist Threat Integration Center, we will embrace the opportunities and challenges it presents.

//Signed//
George J. Tenet

cc: ADCI/US, Winston P. Wiley

Attachment:
MOU on Information Sharing

MEMORANDUM OF UNDERSTANDING BETWEEN THE INTELLIGENCE COMMUNITY, FEDERAL LAW ENFORCEMENT AGENCIES, AND THE DEPARTMENT OF HOMELAND SECURITY CONCERNING INFORMATION SHARING

This Agreement provides a framework and guidance to govern information sharing, use, and handling between: the Secretary of Homeland Security, on behalf of the Department of Homeland Security (DHS), including all entities that are or become, wholly or in part, elements of DHS; the Director of Central Intelligence (DCl), on behalf of all entities that are, or become, wholly or in part, elements of the United States Intelligence Community (IC), other than those that are to become part of DHS; and the Attorney General, on behalf of the Department of Justice (DOJ), including the Federal Bureau of Investigation, and all entities that are, or become, wholly or in part, elements of DOJ, and any other department, agency, or entity having federal law enforcement responsibilities, other than those that are to become part of DHS.

I.   Scope of Application. This Agreement shall be binding on all such departments, agencies, and entities on whose behalf the Secretary of Homeland Security, the DCl, and the Attorney General agree herein. This Agreement is intended to mandate minimum requirements and procedures for information sharing, use, and handling, and for coordination and deconfliction of analytic judgments. Departments and agencies are encouraged to develop additional procedures and mechanisms to provide for greater information sharing and coordination than required herein, consistent with the DHS Legislation and other relevant statutory authorities, Presidential Directives, the President's announced policies for protecting against terrorist threats to the homeland, and this Agreement, including, but not limited to:

(a) the Homeland Security Act of 2002;
(b) the National Security Act of 1947, as amended;
(c) the Uniting and Strengthening America by Providing Appropriate Tools Required to Intercept and Obstruct Terrorism Act of 2001;
(d) the Foreign Intelligence Surveillance Act, as amended;
(e) Executive Order 12333, as amended, and any subsequent Executive Orders on Intelligence Activities;
(f) Executive Order 13231, as amended, and any subsequent Executive Orders on Homeland Security;
(g) Guidelines Regarding Disclosure to the Director of Central Intelligence and Homeland Security Officials of Foreign Intelligence Acquired in the Course of a Criminal Investigation, dated September 23. 2002; and
(h) Guidelines for Disclosure of Grand Jury and Electronic. Wire, and Oral Interception Information Identifying United States Persons, dated September 23, 2002.

To the extent that this Agreement provides for more expansive information sharing than other authorities or agreements, with the exception of statutes, or Presidential Directives including, but not limited to. Executive Orders, ("Presidential Directives"), the more expansive provisions of this Agreement shall be followed

2.   Definitions. For purposes of this Agreement:

(a)   "Analytic conclusion" means the product of analysis of one or more pieces of information in which inferences are drawn from the information being analyzed to arrive at a determination about a fact - such as, for example, a potential threat - that is not explicit or apparent from the face of the original information itself. It does not include, for example, a summary of the factual content of a piece of intelligence information, a report of an interview, or a report or other document that merely collects and summarizes information from multiple sources about the same or related topics, or other types of communication which do not include analytic conclusions as described above.

(b)   "Attorney General" means the Attorney General of the United States or the Attorney General's designee, except as otherwise provided herein.

(c)   "Classified information" means information that has been determined pursuant to Executive Order No. 12958, or any successor order, Executive Order No. 12951, or any successor order, or the Atomic Energy Act of 1954 (42 U.S.C. 2011), to require protection against unauthorized disclosure.

(d)   "Covered entity" means: any department, agency, bureau, office or other entity that is, or becomes, wholly or in part, an element of the Department of Homeland Security (including the Department itself); any department, agency, bureau, office or other entity that is, or becomes, wholly or in part, an element of the United States Intelligence Community or the Department of Justice; and any other department, agency, or entity having federal law enforcement responsibilities.

(e)   "Covered information" means terrorism information, weapons of mass destruction (WMD) information, vulnerabilities information, and other information relevant to the duties of the Department of Homeland Security, as well as analyses based wholly or in part on such covered information.

(f)   "Department" or "DHS" shall mean the Department of Homeland Security and any entity that is, or becomes, an element of that Department.

(g)   "DHS Legislation" means the Homeland Security Act of 2002 (H.R. 5005, 107th Congress, 2d Session) (November 26, 2002), as it may be amended from'time to time.

(h)   "DCI" means the Director of Central Intelligence, or, except as otherwise provided herein, the DCl's designee, in his or her capacity as head of the Intelligence Community, and as head of the Central Intelligence Agency.

(i)   "Foreign intelligence" has the meaning given to that term in section 3 of the National Security Act of 1947. as amended (50 U.S.C. 401 a), as that statutory term may be amended from time to time.

(j)   "Homeland" means the United States as defined in the DHS Legislation.

(k)   "Infrastructure" means the basic systems, assets, facilities, services, and installations needed for the functioning of our society. The term includes, but is not limited to, critical infrastructure, meaning systems and assets, whether physical or virtual, so vital to the United States that the incapacity or destruction of such systems and assets would have a debilitating impact on United States national security, economic security, national public health or safety, or any combination of these. Critical infrastructure includes, but is not limited to, agriculture, food, water, public health, emergency services, government, defense industrial base, information and telecommunications, energy, transportation, banking and finance, chemical industry and hazardous materials, postal and shipping, and national monuments and icons.

(l)   "Infrastructure information" means all information related to the identification, status, security, criticality, risk assessment, vulnerability to ail means of attack, interdependency, and attack consequences (including potential impact on public health or safety, the economy, national security, governance and public confidence) of the infrastructure of the United States.

(m)   "Intelligence Community" has the meaning given it in section 3(4) of the National Security Act of 1947 (50 U.S.C. 40la(4)), as it may be amended from time to time.

(n)   "Need-to-know" means a determination made by an authorized holder of classified information, or sensitive law enforcement information, that a prospective recipient requires access to a specific piece, or category of information in order to perform or assist in a lawful and authorized governmental function.

(o)   "Parties" means the signatories to this Agreement and their successors, on behalf of all covered entities they head, supervise or represent.

(p)   "PATRIOT Act" means the Uniting and Strengthening America by Providing Appropriate Tools Required to Intercept and Obstruct Terrorism (USA PATRIOT) Act of 2001, Pub L. 107-56, 115 StaL 272,278-81.

(q)   "Secretary" means the Secretary of Homeland Security or the Secretary's designee, execpt as otherwise provided herein.

(r)   "Terrorism information" means all information relating to the existence, organization, capabilities, plans, intentions, vulnerabilities, means of finance or material support, or activities of foreign or international terrorist groups or individuals, domestic groups or individuals involved in terrorism, to threats posed by such groups or individuals to the United States, United States persons, or United States interests, or to those of other nations, or to communications between such groups or individuals, and to information relating to groups or individuals reasonably believed to be assisting or associated with then).

(s)   "Vulnerabilities information" means all information relating to the susceptibility - actual, perceived, or conceptual - of the United States, including any portion, sector, population, geographic area, or industry, to terrorist attack.

(t)   "Weapons of Mass Destruction information" or "WMD information" means terrorism information or vulnerabilities information relating to conventional explosive weapons and non-conventional weapons capable of causing mass casualties and damage, including chemical or biological agents, radioactive or nuclear materials, and the means to deliver them.

3.   <u>Policies and Procedures for Information Sharing, Handling and Use.</u> Consistent with the DHS Legislation, and except as otherwise specifically provided in this Agreement, the following

agreed-upon policies and procedures shall apply to the provision of covered information by any covered entity to any other covered entity, to the interpretation of all provisions of this Agreement, and to the resolution of all issues related to information sharing, handling and use, and the coordination and deconfliction of operations and analytic conclusions:

(a) *Priority on Preemption, Prevention, and Disruption.* All procedures, guidelines, and mechanisms under this Agreement shall be designed and implemented, and all determinations with regard to sharing information covered by this Agreement shall be made, with the understood, overriding priority of preventing, preempting, and disrupting terrorist threats to our homeland. The parties recognize and agree that, in some cases, this priority shall dictate information sharing even where doing so may affect criminal prosecutions or ongoing law enforcement or intelligence operations. Nonetheless, the covered entities shall act under this Agreement in a manner to protect, to the greatest extent possible, these other significant interests, including the protection of intelligence and sensitive law enforcement sources and methods, other classified information, and sensitive operational and prosecutorial information.

(b) *Reciprocity and Transparency.* All information collected by any covered entity relevant to the missions and responsibilities of any other covered entities should be shared, to the greatest extent possible, between and among all covered entities. Likewise, the parties agree that, to the greatest extent possible, there should be transparency between and among the covered entities with regard to their activities to preempt, prevent, and disrupt terrorist attacks against U.S. persons and interests. Except as otherwise specified in this Agreement, or mandated by relevant Federal statutes or Presidential Directives, procedures and mechanisms for information sharing, use, and handling shall be interpreted and implemented consistently and reciprocally regardless of the role a particular covered entity plays as a provider or recipient of covered information. In other words, for example, international terrorism information collected by the Border Patrol should be shared by DHS with the IC to the same extent foreign intelligence information on terrorism is shared by the IC with DHS.

(c) *Scope of "Covered Information."* Consistent with the priority established in Section 3(a), information relating to terrorism, Weapons of Mass Destruction, vulnerabilities, or other functions of the Department of Homeland Security shall be presumed to be "covered information" under this Agreement. If, after applying this presumption, disagreement remains between covered entities about whether particular information is "covered information," such disagreement shall be resolved pursuant to Section 4(d).

(d) *Effective date of information sharing obligations.* Notwithstanding provisions of this Agreement mandating further agreement on mechanisms, procedures, or other issues, the parties recognize that the obligation to promptly begin the full range of information sharing mandated by the DHS Legislation came into force on January 24, 2003, and that obligations under this Agreement will be in force upon the signature of all parties.

(e) *Sharing Requirements Based on Substance Only.* Consistent with the DHS Legislation and other relevant statutory authorities, Presidential Directives, the President's announced policies for protecting against terrorist threats to the homeland, and this Agreement, the parties agree that this Agreement requires that covered information, including, but not limited to, terrorism information, WMD information, infrastructure, and vulnerabilities information, be provided by any covered entity that collects or analyzes that information to any other covered entity that has a need-to-know that information (or information relating to that subject matter), based on a broad interpretation of the mission of the other covered entity, regardless of:

(i) <u>The type of communication in which the information is incorporated.</u> Covered information must be provided as required in this Agreement regardless of the type of communication in which it is originally reported by the providing agency. The fact that particular covered information may be contained originally in a particular type of communication shall not, under any circumstances, be grounds either to withhold or delay the sharing of any covered information. As illustrative examples only, covered information must be provided by CIA, within the time frames agreed to, whether such information is contained originally in communications referred to as "TDs," "intel cables," "ops cables," or any other type of communication. Likewise, covered information must be provided by the FBI, within the time frames agreed to, whether such information is contained originally in communications referred to as "302s," "ECs," "LHMs," or any other type of communication;

(ii) <u>The manner in which the information is or may be conveyed to the intended agency or individual recipients.</u> Covered entities shall continually endeavor to improve technological means of access to afford maximum flexibility, speed, and volume of information shared, consistent with the strictly necessary protection of intelligence or sensitive law enforcement sources and methods, and with section 3(a) and other relevant provisions of this Agreement.

(f) *Terrorist Threat Integration Center.* The parties agree that, when fully operational, the Terrorist Threat Integration Center (TTIC) shall be the preferred, though not the exclusive, method for sharing covered.information at the national level. TTIC information-sharing mechanisms and procedures shall be consistent with the DHS Legislation and other relevant statutory authorities, Presidential Directives, the President's announced policies for protecting against terrorist threats to the homeland, and this Agreement. As soon as practicable, the parties shall determine the extent to which provision of information to one or more covered entities via the TTIC may constitute the only required method for providing such information to such entities, provided however, that any.decision to share covered information among the parties solely by means of the TTIC shall be memorialized in a separate written agreement executed by the parties, including by designees of the officials signing this Agreement. Analytic conclusions contained in TTIC products shall not be altered by agencies prior to dissemination.

(g) *Policies for Sharing Particular Types of Information With DHS.* Consistent with the DHS Legislation and other relevant statutory authorities, Presidential Directives, the President's announced policies for protecting against terrorist threats to the homeland, and this Agreement, the Secretary shall be provided access to all information necessary for him to carry out the mission of the Department. Except as otherwise directed by the President, the parties agree that the amount of information and depth of detail of information provided to the Secretary, which will vary by the type of information at issue, will be governed by the following policies:

(I) <u>Information Related to Threats of Terrorism Against the United States.</u> As required by the DHS Legislation, DHS shall be provided, without request, all "reports (including information reports containing intelligence which has not been fully evaluated), assessments, and analytical information." The parties understand that, in this category, except upon further request by DHS, and agreement by the originating entity, provided information will not routinely include information, collected through intelligence sources or methods, or sensitive law enforcement sources or methods, which has not been processed in any way to reduce the amount of substantive content or synthesize the material. Thus, for example, a recording of a conversation intercepted under the Foreign Intelligence Surveillance Act (FISA) or an intelligence officer's or FBI agent's hand-written notes of a discussion with a source would not be routinely provided in thiis category. By contrast, a report forwarding the substance of a FISA-recorded conversation, or an FBI "Electronic Communication" (EC), including the substance of a discussion with a source, even if these include verbatim quotes from the underlying notes, would be provided. ECs containing substantive information, along with "302s," "TDs," "IIRs," and all other similar documents including substantive information, fall into the category of information to be provided. The parties agree, as soon as practicable, to identity and/or put into place necessary and reasonable mechanisms, including, when operational, the TTIC, along with the Joint Terrorism Task Forces (JTTFs), and procedures, to ensure that DHS receives all such information automatically, under the policies and procedures agreed to in this Agreement, without further request.

(ii)   Vulnerabilities Information. As required by the DHS Legislation, DHS shall be provided, without request, all information of any kind concerning "the vulnerability of the infrastructure of the United States, or other vulnerabilities of the United States, to terrorism, whether or not such information has been analyzed." The parties understand that, in this category, without further request by DHS, provided information will routinely include information, collected through intelligence sources or methods, or sensitive law enforcement sources or methods, which has not been processed in any way to reduce the amount of substantive content or synthesize the material. Provided information will include all types of information, without regard to the distinctions drawn by way of example in Section 3(g)(i), except as further agreed to by the parties or their designees. The parties agree, as soon as practicable, to identify and/or put into place necessary and reasonable mechanisms, including, when operational, the TTIC, along with the JTTFs, and procedures, to ensure that DHS receives all such information, under the principles agreed to in this Agreement, without further request.

(iii)   Information Relating to Significant and Credible Threats of Terrorism. As required by the DHS Legislation, DHS shall be provided, without request, all information of any kind concerning "significant and credible threats of terrorism against the United States, whether or not such information has been analyzed." The parties understand that, in this category, without further request by DHS, provided information will routinely include information, collected through intelligence sources or methods, or sensitive law enforcement sources or methods, which has not been processed in any way to reduce the amount of substantive content or synthesize the material. Provided information will include all types of information, without regard to the distinctions drawn by way of example in Section 3(g)(i), except as further agreed to by the parties or their designees. The parties agree, as soon as practicable, to identify and/or put into place neccssary and reasonable mechanisms, including, when operational, the TTIC, along with the JTTFs, and procedures, to ensure that DHS receives all such information, under the principles agreed to in this Agreement, without further request.

(iv)   Other Information Requested by the Secretary. The Secretary shall be provided, upon request, with such other information relating to threats of terrorism against the United States or to other areas of DHS' responsibility, whether or not such information has been analyzed. The parties understand that DHS will be provided information in this category upon request including, if so requested, information which has not been processed in any way to reduce the amount of substantive content or synthesize the material. If so requested, provided information will include all types of information, without regard to the distinctions drawn by way of example in Section 3(g)(i), except as otherwise directed by the President. The parties agree, as soon as practicable, to set up necessary and reasonable mechanisms, including, when operational, the TtlC, along with the JTTFs, and procedures, to ensure that DHS, when requested, receives all such information, under the principles agreed to in this Agreement.

(h)   *Timely Sharing of Information.* Covered information must be provided to those with a need-to-know that information (or information relating to that subject matter), based on a broad interpretation of the mission of the other covered entity, as quickly as possible. Providing all timely and relevant covered information to those who have a need-to-know it in order to assist them in meeting their homeland security-related responsibilities is fundamental to the succcss of the Department and all other efforts to ensure the security of the homeland from terrorist attack. Delay in providing such information risks frustrating efforts to meet these critical responsibilities and could result in preventable attacks against U.S. persons or interests failing to be preempted, prevented, or disrupted. Accordingly, except as otherwise directed by the President or agreed to by all parties, the parties agree that:

(i)   Information that a covered entity reasonably believes relates to a potential terrorism or WMD threat, to the United States homeland, its infrastructure, or to United States persons or interests, shall be provided immediately to other covered entities;

(ii)   Other covered information, including, but not limited to, vulnerabilities information, but which a covered entity does not reasonably believe relates to a potential terrorism or WMD threat to the United States homeland, its infrastructure, or to United States persons or interests, shall be provided as expeditiously as possible;

(iii)   Under no circumstances may covered information be withheld from a covered entity with a need-to-know that information (or information relating to that subject matter), based on a broad interpretation of the mission of the other covered entity, or may the sharing of such information be delayed beyond the time frames agreed to in this Agreement, except as consistent with the Section 4(d), or other relevant provisions of this Agreement;

(iv)   When a question arises as to whether covered information must be provided to the Department or any other covered entity pursuant to this; Agreement, the parties will resolve the question pursuant to Section 4(d);

(v)   Covered entities agree to use, to the greatest extent possible, the most rapid methods of information sharing, consistent with the strictly necessary protection of intelligence or sensitive law enforcement sources and methods, and with Section 3(a) and other relevant provisions of this Agreement; and

(vi)   Consistent with Section 3, and other relevant provisions of this Agreement, the parties agree that they shall work diligently to ensure that all covered entities receive the same information within the same time frame. Agreement, to withhold in its entirety a communication containing covered information, such indication shall occur immediately.

(v)   The parties agree that the provisions of this section shall-not apply to established source protection procedures utilized by CIA's Directorate of Operations, or equivalent procedures developed and used by other covered entities, provided that such procedures do not result in the failure to provide DHS with substantive information as required under the DHS Legislation and this Agreement, and that the Secretary may personally request revisions in such procedures if he detennines that they restrict DHS' access to information in a way that jeopardizes DHS' mission. For information described in Section 3(i)(i), such procedures shall be revised, as soon as is practicable, and without request from the Secretary, to ensure that those procedures'only remove such intelligence that clearly identifies, or would reasonably permit ready identification of, intelligence or sensitive law enforcement sources or methods that are particularly susceptible to countermeasures that would nullify or measurably rcduce their effectiveness.

(j)   *Requests for Additional Information.* In addition to the participation of DHS in the "requirements" processes, as discussed further herein, the DHS Legislation provides for DHS to request additional or follow-up information upon receipt of individual items of information. As soon as practicable, the parties shall agree to mechanisms and procedures, including the TTIC, JTTFs, and, if appropriate, focal points, for DHS to make, and covered entities to respond to, such requests. These mechanisms and procedures shall be designed to facilitate the greatest amount of additional information sharing consistent with strictly necessary protection of intelligence, or sensitive law enforcement sources and methods, with Section 3(a) and other relevant provisions of this Agreement, and with the timeliest possible responses to requests for additional information.

(k)   *Information Use Restrictions.* In general, parties shall disclose covered information free of any originator controls or information use restrictions. Several categories of covered information that must be disclosed to covered entities pursuant to the DHS Legislation, this Agreement, and other authorities, remain subject to special labeling, handling, storage, use and access auditing requirements imposed by statute or, to the extent consistent with the DHS Legislation, Presidential Directives, the President's announced policies for protecting against terrorist threats to the homeland, and this Agreement, pursuant to applicable regulations. The scope and duration of such restrictions, including caveats restricting use of the disclosed information to a particular level or element of a covered entity, will be tailored to address the particular situation or subject matter involved. When imposed, use restrictions shall be no more restrictive than strictly necessary to accomplish the desired effect.

(l)   *Secondary Information Sharing.* To the extent consistent with this Agreement, covered entities may share information provided by other covered entities with additional covered entities. Such secondary sharing shall be carried out, to the greatest extent possible, in a manner that permits the originating agency to know to whom the information has been provided. The parties shall agree, as soon as is practicable, upon recommendations, if any, for changes to Executive Order 12958, Director of Centrai Intelligence Directive 6/6 (and complementary or successor directives dealing with Originator Controls, the so-called "third agency rule," and other policies or procedures governing the sharing of received information with additional recipients) in order to comply with the DHS Legislation, and to carry out the President's announced policies for protecting against terrorist threats to the homeland, and the provisions of this Agreement.

(m)   *Other Obligations to Share Information.* A covered entity's voluntary or obligatory provision of covered information to another covered entity does not in itself discharge or diminish any other obligation the providing entity may have to provide that information, or any part of it, to any other department, agency or other public or private organization or individual under any statute, Presidential Directive, or other agreement.

Although all covered entities will attempt to identify and call attention to information relevant to the mission of other covered entities, the responsibility to share information relevant to the mission or responsibilities of any covered entity in addition to DHS remains the responsibility of the originator or initial federal recipient of the information and does not shift to DHS by virtue of DHS' receipt of the information. The parties agree, however, that, to the greatest extent possible, other sharing obligations shall be harmonized and coordinated with those covered by this Agreement, including the agreed preference for using the TTIC and JTFFs as information-sharing mechanisms, in order to reduce duplication, facilitate deconfliction, and increase efficiency.

(n)   *PATRIOT Act Information.* Law enforcement-related information related to DHS mission, permitted or required to be provided to intelligence agencies under the PATRIOT Act and its implementing guidelines shall also be considered covered information under this Agreement and shall, therefore, be provided to the Department and other covered entities, in accordance with the DHS Legislation and other relevant statutory provisions, and this Agreement.

(o)   *Other Intelligence Information.* Nothing in this Agreement shall be read to restrict the access of the Secretary or his designee to information the Secretary ordinarily would receive as a member of the Intelligence Community, including national security and foreign intelligence information.

(p)   *Information Sharing Mechanisms.* As soon as practicable, the parties shall agree upon specific mechanisms, consistent with Section 3 and other relevant provisions of this Agreement, for how different types of covered information will be shared, including technical and administrative arrangements, and, as appropriate, designation of focal points, to maximize the effectiveness and coordination for providing covered information. Subsequent arrangements for information sharing may he reached upon the approval of the parties or their designees. The parties shall work to develop, as part of this process, effective mcchanisms for covered entities to identify covered information held by them and to ensure, to the greatest degree feasible, the provision of such information, without specific request, to other covered entities. The parties further agree that, notwithstanding their agreement to develop further mechanisms and procedures for information sharing, covered entities shall promptly build on mechanisms and procedures already in place to identify and provide to DHS covered information that is generated or received by them in the course of carrying out their missions.

(q)   *Methods of Providing Information.* The parties recognize and agree that there are many possible methods for "providing" information, including, but not limited to, hand-delivery, oral briefings, transmission by secure data-link, and affording routine and unrestricted access to computerized databases, including the ability to transfer such information to a recipient entity as neccssary, and by full and complete co-location of analysts or other personnel and full integration of, and access to, information, as well as, for example, ensuring that the Secretary receives all daily threat briefing materials (including threat matrices and overnight reports). The parties further agree that requirements to "provide" information under this Agreement may be satisfied, depending on the type of information at issue, by the use of a single mechanism, such as via the TTIC, consistent with section 3(f) of this Agreement, or a combination of mechanisms already in place and/or created under this Agreement. The parties shall agree, as part of the development of these mcchanisms and procedures, as to which method, or combination of methods, of providing information will be sufficient for particular types or categories of information.

(r)   *Responsible Officials for Information Sharing.* Until such time as modified by the parties, the responsible officials tor information sharing under this Agreement are as follows:

(i)   For the Secretary of Homeland Security, the Undersecretary for Information Analysis and Infrastructure Protection, or another individual designated by the Secretary to act in this capacity;

(ii)   For the Attorney General, Executive Assistant Director for Counterterrorism and Counterintelligence; and

(iii)   For the Director of Central Intelligence, the Associate Director of Central Intelligence for Homeland Security.

(s)   *Provision of Covered Information to the DHS Directorate of Information Analysis and Infrastructure Protection.* Until further agreement by the parties, or their designees, all covered information provided, including information provided, under current procedures, to existing elements transferred to DHS, e.g., the United States Coast Guard and the U.S. Customs Service, shall also be separately provided to the Directorate of Information Analysis and Infrastructure Protection, including, if agreed by the Secretary, via the TTIC. The Undersecretary for Information Analysis and Infrastructure Protection, or another individual designated by the Sccrctary to act in this capacity, shall work with entities not within the Directorate to ensure effective coordination of information.

(t)   *Classified Information.* The head of each covered entity shall put procedures in place to ensure that each individual recipient of classified information has, and maintains, appropriate security clearances, training, and need-to-know to receive classified information at the level at which the recipient will receive such information, individuals shall be designated at each covered entity at several levels of seniority to receive classified information judged by the originating agency to be sufficiently sensitive to require limited distribution. In rare cases, the parties expect that extremely sensitive information may be provided only to the Secretary or, as appropriate, the head of another covered entity. The head of each covered entity also shall ensure that all mechanisms and procedures for receiving, storing, and handling classified information meet established legal and regulatory standards. The policies and procedures governing access to covered information under this Agreement, including such information that is classified, shall apply without regard to whether that information is made available in written, oral, or electronic form, or to the means or mechanism by which it is communicated to the recipient.

(u)   *Thresholds.* In order to ensure that the Department is provided with all information necessary to carry out its responsibilities, but is not inundated with unmanageable volumes of information below thresholds reasonable to perform its mission, as soon as practicable, the Secretary shall advise the other parties, individually or collectively, as to establishing additional thresholds for information sharing, consistent with the DHS Legislation. For example, the Secretary may determine that low-level information concerning purely indigenous foreign terrorist groups with no apparent capability to mount operations against the United States is not relevant to DHS' mission. Such further agreement shall be consistent with the DHS Legislation and other relevant statutory authorities, Presidential Directives, the President's announced policies for protecting against terrorist threats to the homeland, and this Agreement. At any time following such initial agreement, the parties may agree to additional information sharing, or to more or less restrictive thresholds, as the volume of information involved and the needs of DHS become clearer, so long as such agreements are consistent with the DHS legislation and this Agreement. Such agreements may be made by designees of the parties.

(v)   *Privacy.* All information sharing pursuant to this Agreement shall be consistent with applicable privacy laws.

4.   **Coordination, Deconfliction, and Dispute Resolution.**

(a)   *Coordination and Deconjliciion Policy.* Consistent with the President's direction that our highest priority is the protection of the American people from potentially devastating terrorist attacks, covered entities shall take all necessary measures to ensure that terrorist threats to our homeland are addressed cooperatively, efficiently, and with the understood overriding purpose of preventing, preempting, and disrupting those threats. To that end, the parties agree that no homeland security-related prevention, preemption, or disruption activity of any covered entity shall be presumed to be the best option in any given case, or otherwise deemed of higher precedence, importance, or priority than any other such activity. The covered entities shall work together, to the greatest extent possible, to achieve, in each case, the maximum preventative, preemptive, and disruptive effect on potential threats, including coordinating simultaneous and complementary activities of multiple covered entities when appropriate. Because the failure to coordinate operational activities to preempt, prevent, and disrupt terrorist threats can create confusion, inefficiency and, in extreme cases, dangerous situations resulting from conflicting operational activities, the parties agree to coordinate operational activities to the greatest possible extent. Specifically, each party shall take all reasonable steps to ensure coordination and deconfliction of homeland security-related law enforcement, intelligence or national security-related activities of covered entities under that party's authority with such activities of other covered entities.

(b)   *Analytic Conclusions and Supporting Information.* Terrorism and other homeland-security related analytic efforts of all covered entities must be informed by the most comprehensive, accurate, and timely information available, regardless of its nature and source, including, but not limited to, terrorism, WMD, vulnerabilities, and other pertinent information available to any covered entity. Analytic conclusions relating to terrorist or WMD threats to the homeland, or other issues within the responsibility of DHS, including information updating and amplifying previous conclusions, must be shared with all covered entities as soon as they are produced. Preemptive, preventative, and disruptive actions by all covered entities must be informed to the greatest extent possible by all available information and by all analytic conclusions, including.competing conclusions, of all entities with relevant analytic responsibilities. At the same time, the Federal government must, to the greatest extent possible, speak with one voice to state and local officials, private industry, and the public, in order to prevent confusion, mixed signals, and, potentially, dangerous operational conflicts. In furtherance of these goals, the parties agree as follows:

(i)   The parties shall ensure that covered entities disseminate their terrorism or other homeland security-related analytic products without delay to other covered entities that have related interests and responsibilities;

(ii)   Except as otherwise provided in Sections 4(bXiii) or (iv), no analytic conclusions, as defined in Section 2(a) of this Agreement, of any covered entity shall be disseminated to state, local, or private sector officials, or to the public, without the prior approval of the Secretary of Homeland Security, his designee, or in accordance with approval mechanisms, potentially including the TTIC or the JTTFs, established by the Secretary after the date of this Agreement.

(iii) Analytic conclusions may be provided directly to such officials or to the public where the head of a covered entity or his or her designee reasonably determines that exigent circumstances exist such that providing an analytic conclusion prior to required approval is necessary to prevent, preempt, or disrupt an imminent threat of death or serious bodily injury or significant damage to U.S. infrastructure or other interests. In the event an analytic conclusion is disseminated pursuant to the exigent circumstances exception in this paragraph, the Secretary and other covered entities shall be notified immediately of the dissemination.

(iv) Analytic conclusions may be shared with federal, state, and local law enforcement officials without the prior approval of the Secretary of Homeland Security, provided, however, that it is the intention of the parties that DHS be provided with the earliest possible advance notice of the potential of such communications and, where possible, DHS will be included in the development of the communications through the DHS liaisons at FBI Headquarters. The Secretary of Homeland Security, or his designee (including a DHS representative to a JTTF if designated by the Secretary to do so), must approve further dissemination of such analytic conclusions to other non-law enforcement state and local officials or to the public.

(v) Nothing in this Agreement shall prevent covered entities from coordinating on analytic conclusions with, or seeking the views of, other Federal Government entities in evaluating terrorism or other homeland-security-related information.

(c) *Establishment of Mechanisms for Operational Coordination and Deconfliction.* As soon as practicable, the parties shall agree upon specific mechanisms, including technical, administrative, and, as appropriate, designation of focal points, to maximize the effectiveness of operational coordination and deconfliction. These will cover both overseas and domestic operations related to homeland security. Subsequent agreements for operational coordination and deconfliction may be reached upon the approval of the parties or their designees.

(d) *Information Sharing Dispute Resolution.* Consistent with the DHS Legislation and other relevant statutory authorities, Presidential Directives, the President's announced policies for protecting against terrorist threats to the homeland, the obligation to protect intelligence or sensitive law enforcement sources and methods firom unauthorized disclosure, and with Section 3(a), and other relevant sections of this Agreement, issues concerning the application of the terms of this Agreement in any specific context with respect to whether particular covered information should be provided to the Department or to any other covered entity shall be handled under the following procedures:

(i) A holder of particular covered information at issue, whether within or outside the entity originating that information, shall refer the matter by the most expeditious means to the head of the entity originating the information (or that official's designee) for expeditious review.

(ii) The reviewing official shall, without exception, render a definitive decision on the request within 24 hours of receiving the referral and, in light of the access provisions in the DHS Legislation, shall resolve any doubt in favor of providing the requested information.

(iii)   If the originating agency's reviewing official declines to provide the covered information requested, that official shall, within the 24 hours allotted for response, provide the Department or other covered with —

   (A)   the fact that the specific information is being withheld;

   (B)   a succinct and specific statement of the reasons for the withholding; and

   (C)   as much of the information requested as the head of the originating agency (or that official's designee) reasonably concludes can be provided given the President's announced policies for protecting against terrorist threats to the homeland, the DHS Legislation and other relevant statutory authorities, and relevant Presidential Directives.

(iv)   If, at that point, a compromise is not reached expeditiously, the dispute will be resolved either by the Secretary, Attorney General, and DCI by mutual decision or through referral to the Assistant to the President for National Security Affairs and Assistant to the President for Homeland Security Affairs, or their designees, for resolution. Notwithstanding any other provision of this Agreement, the Attorney General, Secretary, or DCI, or their deputies may, whenever any of them deems it necessary or advisable (particularly when a fundamental matter of policy is implicated or time is of the essence), intervene to raise and resolve any issue of access to covered information by mutual decision or through the National Security Council and/or Homeland Security Council system.

(e)   *NSPD-8*. Nothing in this Agreement in any way affects the responsibilities and authorities for coordination of United Slates counter-terrorism activities established in National Security Presidential Directive (NSPD) 8.

5.   *Protection of Intelligence and Sensitive Law Enforcement Sources and Methods.* The parties intend that all provisions of this Agreement be interpreted consistently with the DCI's statutory responsibility to protect intelligence sources and methods from unauthorized disclosure and with similar responsibilities of the Attorney General and the Secretary to protect sensitive law enforcement sources and methods, with the DHS Legislation and other relevant statutory authorities, Presidential Directives, the President's announced policies for protecting against terrorist threats to the homeland, and with Scction 3(a), and other relevant provisions of this Agreement. Consistent with this agreed-upon interpretation:

(a)   The DCI shall carry out his responsibilities for the protection of intelligence sources and methods, and the Secretary and Attorney General shall carry out analogous responsibilities for sensitive law enforcement sources and methods, in a manner, and through mechanisms, that ensure that all covered information is made available promptly to the Department, and to other covered entities with a need-to-know and proper security clearances and handling procedures in place, subject only to such handling and use restrictions as are strictly and unavoidably necessary to protect intelligence and sensitive law enforcement sources and methods from unauthorized disclosure.

   (I)   The DCI shall ensure that the substance of all covered information relevant to the responsibilities of all covered entities is provided to those entities in a form suited to their effective use of that information, consistent with the DCI's obligation to protect intelligence sources and methods from unauthorized disclosure and Section 3(a) of this Agreement. The Secretary and the Attorney General shall similarly ensure that the substance of covered information is provided in a suitable form.

(ii)   The DCI shall ensure that dissemination of classified reporting based, wholly or in part, on covered information, is accompanied by dissemination of as much of that reporting and covered information as is possible at an unclassified (which may, when necessary, be marked "Sensitive-but-Unclassified" or "SBU") or reduced classification level, in order to ensure the broadest possible availability and use of covered information by those with a need-to-know that information (or information relating to that subject matter), based on a broad interpretation of the mission of the other covered entity.; The Secretary and the Attorney General shall similarly ensure that dissemination is done in a manner that ensures the broadest possible availability.

(b)   Information may be redacted or put into a tailored product to the extent consistent with Section 3(i) of this Agreement.

(c)   Nothing in this section relieves any member of the Intelligence Community that originates covered information from its obligation to provide that information to DHS and other covered entities, as appropriate, in a form consistent with this Agreement, the DHS Legislation, and other relevant statutes and authorities regarding the protection of sources and methods.

6. "Sanitization" and Modification of Classification Levels for Further Sharing by DHS.

(a) Consistent with the President's announced policies, our national priorities, including this section. Section 3(a), and other relevant provisions of this Agreement, the DHS Legislation and other relevant statutes and Presidential Directives, covered entities that originate covered information that is classified shall retain the authority to determine whether that information, or any portions thereof, must remain classified in the interest of national security.

(i)   Covered entities shall ensure that covered information that is classified or otherwise subject to restricted dissemination, but which reasonably appears likely to require onward passage to state, local, or private sector officials, the public, or other law enforcement officials for use in a criminal investigation, reaches DHS promptly with accompanying high-content "tear lines" suitable for onward passage at an unclassified level. Until this can be achieved simultaneously to the transmission of covered information, the development of such tearlines shall not delay the provision of covered information.

(ii)   The parties shall ensure, to the greatest extent possible, that covered entities utilize agreed-upon standardized formatting for preparation of tear-line material for passage to state, local, or private sector officials, including state and local law enforcement officials for use in a law enforcement investigation, or to the public, with the goal of providing necessary substantive information, but not enabling recipients to determine the originator, within the Federal government, of the information.

(b) DHS may, on its own initiative or at the request of a homeland security official to whom covered information is disseminated, ask that the originating agency declassify or reduce the classification level attached to that information in order to permit dissemination to additional officials who have a need-to-know the information, to promote ease of handling by those authorized to review it, to permit its incorporation into a document that is unclassified or classified at a lower level, or for other purposes consistent with the need promptly to provide homeland security officials with all relevant covered information that they have a need-to-know in the conduct of their official duties.

Whenever it receives such a request, the originating agency shall respond to DHS, within 24 hours (or such longer period as is agreed to by all parties), unless compelling circumstances exist to require a longer response time. Such response will either —

      (i)   agree to declassify or reduce the classification ievel of the covered information in question as requested; or

      (ii)   provide an alternative formulation responsive to the requester's need for additional information sharing, but without declassifying or reducing the classification of the original document or covered information where that cannot be done consistent with assuring the national security.

(c) Where the need by DHS for further dissemination of classified information received from other covered entities, including through declassification or the preparation of unclassified tear-lines, is urgent because that information contains or may contain terrorist threat indications critical to the ability of homeland security officials to prevent, preempt, or disrupt a possible terrorist attack, that information may be passed directly to the entity or official that has a need-to-know that information, provided that the covered entity passing the information first notifies the originating agency and takes steps reasonable under the exigent circuinstances to protect whatever classified information is not essential to initiating the urgent homeland security assurance measures that may be required.

(d) The parties agree to develop together, as soon as practicable, mechanisms and procedures, including through the use of detailees and assignees to the TTIC and JITFs, as appropriate, to carry out the provisions of Section 6. The parties agree to work together to ensure that the administrative, financial, and personnel burdens of this section are shared to the greatest extent possible among covered entities.

7.   <u>Detail or Assignment of Personnel.</u> To facilitate the information sharing, coordination, and deconfliction policies covered in this Agreement, covered entities shall detail, and/or assign, to the greatest extent possible, including to the TTIC and/or JTTFs, personnel who have the authority either to make classification review and redaction decisions themselves, or, consistent with the time frames established in this Agreement, to refer those decisions to the appropriate officials at the originating agency for prompt action.

8.   <u>DHS Participation in Requirements Processes.</u> As soon as practicable, the parties shall modify existing mechanisms and processes for prioritization of terrorism, WMD and other relevant foreign intelligence collection (including within the United States) and requirements processes to ensure that DHS has meaningful participation at each stage and level of each such mechanism or process, including through participation in the TTIC. The parties also shall work together to provide recommendations as to whether, and how, processes or mechanisms for purely "domestic" terrorism (e.g., concerning the capabilities, plans and intentions of exclusively domestic white supremacist or militia groups), and other relevant intelligence collection should be created or, alternatively, how to ensure meaningful participation by DHS in the prioritization for gathering such information. This section does not refer to operational activities.

9.   <u>Databases.</u> The parties agree to establish procedures and mechanisms to provide DHS, and, as appropriate and practicable, other covered entities, with acccss to databases containing covered information. To this end, the parties shall establish a working group, within 30 days of the date of this Agreement. Developed procedures and mechanisms, including through the use of the TTIC and/or

JTTFs, should be consistent with the DHS Legislation and other relevant statutory authorities, Presidential Directives, the President's announced policies for protecting against terrorist threats to the homeland, and the appropriate needs for access by DHS to appropriate databases, as well as with the protection of intelligence or sensitive law enforcement sources and methods, and with Section 3(a) and other provisions of this Agreement Such procedures and mechanisms should facilitate, to the greatest possible extent: ease and speed of information exchange; differentiated access, to allow individuals with different levels of security clearance and need-to-know to have different levels of access to databases; and compatibility with other databases of covered entities.

10. <u>Statement of Intent Concerning Information Technology.</u> It is the intent of the parties to build and modernize all relevant databases and other information technology systems in order to maximize compatibility with other systems wnh which they must interact. Such procedures and mechanisms also must comply with existing statutory and Presidential Directives, including with regard to the protection of classified information and applicable privacy protections

11. <u>Handling and Storage.</u> The parties shall ensure that covered entities within their jurisdiction observe the established handling and storage standards appropriate to the classification and access restrictions indicated on covered information they receive, use, and disseminate, subject only to the provisions of this Agreement pertaining to exigent circumstances.

12. <u>Information collected and shared by foreign governments.</u> This Agreement contemplates a separate Memorandum of Understanding, consistent with this Agreement, being agreed to by the parties, that addresses concerns related to information collected and shared by foreign governments.

13. <u>Implementation.</u>

(a) Each of the parties shall implement their responsibilities under this Agreement as to the covered entities under their jurisdiction through such binding regulations, orders, directives, and guidance as necessary or prudent from time to time.

(b) Any authonty or duty assigned herein to the Attorney General, the Secretary, or the DCl, may be delegated to one or more subordinate officials at the discretion of the official to whom the authority or duty is assigned, except as otherwise provided in this Agreement. Each such delegation shall be promptly communicated to all other parties.

14. <u>No Private Rights Created.</u> These procedures are not intended to and do not create any rights, privileges, or benefits, substantive or procedural, enforceable by any individual or organization against the United States, its departments, agencies, or other entities, its officers or employees, or any other person.

15. <u>Counterpart Signatures.</u> This Agreement may be signed in counterparts, each of which shall he considered to be an original.

s/s	3-4-03
Attorney General	Date
s/s	MAR 04 2003
Director of Central Intelligence	Date
s/s	Feb. 28 2003
Secretary of Homeland Security	Date

Appedix 6: EXECUTIVE ORDER 13388

Executive Order 13388 of October 25, 2005

Further Strengthening the Sharing of Terrorism Information to Protect Americans

By the authority vested in me as President by the Constitution and the laws of the United States of America, including section 1016 of the Intelligence Reform and Terrorism Prevention Act of 2004 (Public Law 108–458), and in order to further strengthen the effective conduct of United States counterterrorism activities and protect the territory, people, and interests of the United States of America, including against terrorist attacks, it is hereby ordered as follows:

Section 1. *Policy.* To the maximum extent consistent with applicable law, agencies shall, in the design and use of information systems and in the dissemination of information among agencies:

(a) give the highest priority to (i) the detection, prevention, disruption, preemption, and mitigation of the effects of terrorist activities against the territory, people, and interests of the United States of America; (ii) the interchange of terrorism information among agencies; (iii) the interchange of terrorism information between agencies and appropriate authorities of State, local, and tribal governments, and between agencies and appropriate private sector entities; and (iv) the protection of the ability of agencies to acquire additional such information; and

(b) protect the freedom, information privacy, and other legal rights of Americans in the conduct of activities implementing subsection (a).

Sec. 2. *Duties of Heads of Agencies Possessing or Acquiring Terrorism Information.* To implement the policy set forth in section 1 of this order, the head of each agency that possesses or acquires terrorism information:

(a) shall promptly give access to the terrorism information to the head of each other agency that has counterterrorism functions, and provide the terrorism information to each such agency, unless otherwise directed by the President, and consistent with (i) the statutory responsibilities of the agencies providing and receiving the information; (ii) any guidance issued by the Attorney General to fulfill the policy set forth in subsection 1(b) of this order; and (iii) other applicable law, including sections 102A(g) and (i) of the National Security Act of 1947, section 1016 of the Intelligence Reform and Terrorism Prevention Act of 2004 (including any policies, procedures, guidelines, rules, and standards issued pursuant thereto), sections 202 and 892 of the Homeland Security Act of 2002, Executive Order 12958 of April 17, 1995, as amended, and Executive Order 13311 of July 29, 2003; and

(b) shall cooperate in and facilitate production of reports based on terrorism information with contents and formats that permit dissemination that maximizes the utility of the information in protecting the territory, people, and interests of the United States.

Sec. 3. *Preparing Terrorism Information for Maximum Distribution.* To assist in expeditious and effective implementation by agencies of the policy set forth in section 1 of this order, the common standards for the sharing of terrorism information established pursuant to section 3 of Executive Order 13356 of August 27, 2004, shall be used, as appropriate, in carrying out section 1016 of the Intelligence Reform and Terrorism Prevention Act of 2004.

Sec. 4. *Requirements for Collection of Terrorism Information Inside the United States.* To assist in expeditious and effective implementation by agencies of the policy set forth in section 1 of this order, the recommendations regarding the establishment of executive branch-wide collection and sharing requirements, procedures, and guidelines for terrorism information collected within the United States made pursuant to section 4 of Executive Order 13356 shall be used, as appropriate, in carrying out section 1016 of the Intelligence Reform and Terrorism Prevention Act of 2004.

Sec. 5. *Establishment and Functions of Information Sharing Council.*

(a) Consistent with section 1016(g) of the Intelligence Reform and Terrorism Prevention Act of 2004, there is hereby established an Information Sharing Council (Council), chaired by the Program Manager to whom section 1016 of such Act refers, and composed exclusively of designees of: the Secretaries of State, the Treasury, Defense, Commerce, Energy, and Homeland Security; the Attorney General; the Director of National Intelligence; the Director of the Central Intelligence Agency; the Director of the Office of Management and Budget; the Director of the Federal Bureau of Investigation; the Director of the National Counterterrorism Center; and such other heads of departments or agencies as the Director of National Intelligence may designate.

(b) The mission of the Council is to (i) provide advice and information concerning the establishment of an interoperable terrorism information sharing environment to facilitate automated sharing of terrorism information among appropriate agencies to implement the policy set forth in section 1 of this order; and (ii) perform the duties set forth in section 1016(g) of the Intelligence Reform and Terrorism Prevention Act of 2004.

(c) To assist in expeditious and effective implementation by agencies of the policy set forth in section 1 of this order, the plan for establishment of a proposed interoperable terrorism information sharing environment reported under section 5(c) of Executive Order 13356 shall be used, as appropriate, in carrying out section 1016 of the Intelligence Reform and Terrorism Prevention Act of 2004.

Sec. 6. *Definitions.* As used in this order:

(a) the term "agency" has the meaning set forth for the term "executive agency" in section 105 of title 5, United States Code, together with the Department of Homeland Security, but includes the Postal Rate Commission and the United States Postal Service and excludes the Government Accountability Office; and

(b) the term "terrorism information" has the meaning set forth for such term in section 1016(a)(4) of the Intelligence Reform and Terrorism Prevention Act of 2004.

Sec. 7. *General Provisions.*

(a) This order:

(i) shall be implemented in a manner consistent with applicable law, including Federal law protecting the information privacy and other legal rights of Americans, and subject to the availability of appropriations;

(ii) shall be implemented in a manner consistent with the authority of the principal officers of agencies as heads of their respective agencies, including under section 199 of the Revised Statutes (22 U.S.C. 2651), section 201 of the Department of Energy Organization Act (42 U.S.C. 7131), section 103 of the National Security Act of 1947 (50 U.S.C. 403–3), section 102(a) of the Homeland Security Act of 2002 (6 U.S.C. 112(a)), and sections 301 of title 5, 113(b) and 162(b) of title 10, 1501 of title 15, 503 of title 28, and 301(b) of title 31, United States Code;

(iii) shall be implemented consistent with the Presidential Memorandum of June 2, 2005, on "Strengthening Information Sharing, Access, and Integration—Organizational, Management, and Policy Development Structures for Creating the Terrorism Information Sharing

Environment;"
       (iv) shall not be construed to impair or otherwise affect the functions of the Director of the Office of Management and Budget relating to budget, administrative, and legislative proposals; and
       (v) shall be implemented in a manner consistent with section 102A of the National Security Act of 1947.
     (b) This order is intended only to improve the internal management of the Federal Government and is not intended to, and does not, create any rights or benefits, substantive or procedural, enforceable at law or in equity by a party against the United States, its departments, agencies, instrumentalities, or entities, its officers, employees, or agents, or any other person.

Sec. 8. *Amendments and Revocation.*
     (a) Executive Order 13311 of July 29, 2003, is amended:
       (i) by striking "Director of Central Intelligence" each place it appears and inserting in lieu thereof in each such place "Director of National Intelligence"; and
       (ii) by striking "103(c)(7)" and inserting in lieu thereof "102A(i)(1)".
     (b) Executive Order 13356 of August 27, 2004, is hereby revoked.

|signed:|
George W. Bush
THE WHITE HOUSE
October 25, 2005

Appendix 7: DOJ PROTOCOL ON TERRORIST NOMINATIONS

Department of Justice Protocol Regarding Terrorist Nominations

Office of the Deputy Attorney General
Washington, D.C. 20330
October 3, 2008

MEMORANDUM FOR HEADS OF DEPARTMENT COMPONENTS

From: The Deputy Attorney General
Subject: Department of Justice Protocol Regarding Terrorist Walchlist Nominations

The attached protocol reflects a new policy for the Department's internal process for nominating individuals for the Terrorist Screening Database (TSDB).

The TSDB consolidates the U.S. Government's terrorism screening and lookout databases into a single integrated identities database. The TSDB is also known as the "watchlist." This protocol is designed to ensure consistent and appropriate handling of watchlist information. The protocol responds to issues raised by the report of the Inspector General, dated March 14, 2008, entitled "Audit of the U.S. Department of Justice Terrorist Watchlist Nomination Processes." Specifically, that report recommended that the Department adopt a general policy for submission of watch list nominations. Implementation of the attached protocol will accomplish that task.

All components are directed to comply with this protocol effective immediately.

DEPARTMENT OF JUSTICE PROTOCOL
REGARDING TERRORIST WATCHLIST NOMINATIONS

A. Background

1. On September 16, 2003, the President directed the Attorney General in Homeland Security Presidential Directive 6 (HSPD-6) to "establish an organization to consolidate the Government's approach to terrorism screening and provide for the appropriate and lawful use of Terrorist Information in screening processes." Terrorist Information was specifically defined to mean "individuals known or appropriately suspected to be or have been engaged in conduct constituting, in preparation for. in aid of, or related to terrorism."

2. Concurrent with the signing of I ISPD-6, the *Memorandum of Understanding on the Integration and Use of Screening Information to Protect Against Terrorism* (TSC MOU), was signed by the Secretaries of State and Homeland Security, the Attorney General and the Director of Central Intelligence (DCI) (on behalf of the entire U.S. Intelligence Community). The TSC MOU established the Terrorist Screening Center (TSC) to consolidate the Government's approach to terrorism screening and provide for the appropriate and lawful use of Terrorist Information, a term clarified by the inclusion of Terrorist

Identifiers in subsequent agreement of the parties. Under HSPD-6. the TSC was develop and maintain a database, to the extent permitted by law, containing the most thorough, accurate, and current information possible about known or suspected terrorists. HSPD-6 requires that its implementation be consistent with the Constitution and applicable laws, including those protecting the rights of all Americans. The TSC created the Terrorist Screening Database (TSDB) to meet these goals, The TSDB consolidates the U.S. Government's terrorism screening and lookout databases into a single integrated identities database. The TSDB is also known as the "watchlist."

3. The TSC MOU also incorporated all provisions of the *Memorandum of Understanding between the Intelligence Community, Federal Law Enforcement Agencies, and the Department of Homeland Security Concerning Information Sharing,* dated March 4, 2003 (The "Information Sharing MOU").

4. In 2001, the Secretaries of State. Treasury, and Defense became signatories to the Information Sharing MOU by signing Addendum A to the TSC MOU. By doing so, they agreed that all provisions of the TSC MOU and the Information Sharing MOU apply to all entities that are or become a part of their respective Departments.

5. A second addendum (Addendum B), which supplements and incorporates by reference all provisions of the TSC MOU, superseded Addendum A and was finalized on January 18, 2007. The Directors of National Intelligence, NCTC, and the TSC joined as signatories in Addendum B. Under paragraph (1)(b) of Addendum B the Parties agreed, to the maximum extent permitted by law, to "provide to the NCTC on an ongoing basis all Terrorism Information (as defined in the Intelligence Reform and Terrorism Prevention Act (IRTPA) of 2004. Section 1016(a) (4) [as amended to include homeland security information and weapons of mass destruction information] in their possession, custody, or control. Paragraph 7 of Addendum B introduces the term Terrorist Identifiers to more clearly describe the type of terrorism information that NCTC (and the Federal Bureau ol Investigation (FBI) for Purely Domestic Terrorism Information, as defined in the TSC MOU) receives from interagency partners and subsequently shares with TSC for inclusion in the TSDB.

6. Executive Order 13354 (August 27, 2004) created the National Counterterrorism Center (NCTC) to serve as the primary organization in the United States Government for analyzing and integrating all intelligence possessed or acquired by the United States Government pertaining to terrorism and counterterrorism, excepting purely domestic counterterrorism information. That same provision, however, provides that NCTC may receive, retain, and disseminate information from any Federal. State, or local government, or other sourrce necessary to fulfill its responsibilities, giving NCIC authority to receive, retain, and disseminate domestic terrorism informalion.

7. Section 1021 of the Intelligence Reform and Terrorism Prevention Act of 2004 (IRTPA) amended the National Security Act of 1947 to codify the creation of NCTC. Pursuant to IRTPA, NCTC serves "as the central and shared knowledge bank on known and suspected terrorists and international terror groups." NCTC's centralized knowledge bank is known as the Terrorist Identities Datamart Environment (TIDE). Section 1021(c) on Domestic Counterterrorism Intelligence states NCTC "may, consistent with applicable law, the direction of the President, and guidelines referred to in section 102A(b), receive intelligence pertaining exclusively to domestic counterterrorism from any Federal, State, or local government or other sourcc necessary to fulfill its responsibilities and retain and disseminate such intelligence."

8. To enhance information sharing, the President issued Executive Order 13388, *Further Strengthening the Sharing of Terrorism information to Protect Americans* (October 25, 2005), which

requires the head of each agency that possesses or acquires terrorism information to promptly give access to that information to the head of such other agency that has counterterrorism functions.

9. Pursuant to paragraph (2) of HSPD-6, NCTC is mandated to "provide [TSC] with accss to all appropriate information or intelligence in the [NCTC's] custody, possession, or control that [TSC] requires to perform its functions."

10. TIDE serves as the single source for the TSDB, except for Purely Domestic Terrorism Information, which is provided directly to the TSC from the FBI via a formalized procedure. Purely Domestic Terrorism Information is defined in the TSC MOU as "*i.e.,* information about U.S. persons that has been determined to be purely domestic terrorism information with no link to foreign intelligence, counterintelligence, or international terrorism."

11. TIDE contains the identifying and derogatory information on known or appropriately suspected international terrorists and the FBI's Automated Case Support system contains supporting information regarding purely domestic terrorists. The TSDB contains the identifiers exported from TIDE and the identifiers of domestic terrorists exported by the FBI. As it result, the TSDB contains the U.S. Government's comprehensive database of both international and domestic Terrorist Identifiers.

B. Nominating Components

1. The Department of Justice contains a number of components that may acquire information regarding domestic or international terrorists. These components include the FBI, the TSC. the National Security Division, the Criminal Division, the Civil Rights Division, the Drug Enforcement Administration, the United Slates Marshals Service, the Bureau of Alcohol, Tobacco, Firearms, and Explosives, The Federal Bureau of Prisons, the Executive Office of the United States Attorneys, the United States Attorneys, and the United States National Central Bureau.

2. The policy of the Department of Justice is for all components to provide the FBI with all domestic or international Terrorism Information or Terrorist Identifiers so that the FBI can make appropriate nominations to the consolidated terrorist watchlist. With one exception relating to TSC's authority in exigent circumstances, only the FBI is authorized to nominate domestic or international terrorists for inclusion in the TSDB on behalf of the Department of Justice. The FBI has implemented policies governing the submission of such nominations, including procedures to follow when adding, modifying, or deleting a TSDB record, in making any proposed recommendation for watchlisting, each DOJ component should ensure that the underlying information is reasonably accurate, relevant and timely. In addition, the TSC has implemented its *Protocol Regarding; Terrorist Nominations.* These policies must be followed regarding all nominations from the Department of Justice

3. The TSC, which is administered by the FBI and reports to the Attorney General, is permitted to make entries into the TSDB when exigent circumstances exist. Such expedited nominations must be made in compliance with the FBI nomination policies and the TSC's *Protocol Regarding Terrorist Nominations.*

4. The Joint Terrorism Task Forces (JTTF) are a multi-agency effort led by the Department of Justice and the FBI to combine and leverage law enforcement and intelligence community resources to protect the United States from terrorist attack. JTTF's are comprised of highly trained, locally based, investigators, analysts, linguists, and other specialists from Federal, state, local, tribal, territorial law enforcement and intelligence community agencies. The National JTTF was established in July 2002 to serve as the coordinating mechanism for the JTTFs.

5. Department of Justice components, other than the FBI or the TSC. are not permitted to make direct nominations to the TSDB. A Department of Justice component should inform the appropriate JTTF through disseminated intelligence reports, electronic communication, or other method appropriate to the circumstances when it becomes aware of Terrorist Information, Terrorist Identifiers, or Purely Domestic Terrorism Information (collectively, Intelligence Information). The originating DOJ component should state whether it recommends watch listing the individual, the basis for that recommendation, and the investigative steps, if any, it has undertaken regarding the individual. If the JTTF determines that the information received from another component standing alone or in conjunction with other information known to the FBI meets the standards set forth in the Attorney General's Guidelines for opening a preliminary terrorism investigation or a full terrorism investigation and one has not been opened, the JTTF shall initiate an investigation and shall nominate case subjects for inclusion in TIDE and/or the TSDB in accordance with FBI plicy, by forwarding all Intelligence Information, as appropriate, to the FBI's Terrorist Review and Examination Unit (TREX) using the FD-930 form and process.

6. The relevant JTTF will notify the Department of Justice component that Intelligence Information provided by that component has been used, in whole or in part, as the basis for a nomination to the TSDB or the creation of a record in TIDE. To the extent possible, the relevant JTTF will assign a representative from the nominating Department of Justice component to participate in the preliminary or full investigation that arises out of nominations from Department of Justice components. Once notified, the Department component will promptly provide FBI's TREX with additions, modifications, or deletions to a particular record as appropriate regarding that Intelligence Information via the component's JTTF representative.

7. To prevent possible duplicate or partial reporting, the NCTC shall be informed that the FBI and the TSC are the sole TIDE and/or TSDB nominating agencies for the Department of Justice.

8. The provisions of this Protocol are not intended to prejudice, restrict, or interfere with any other agreement or arrangement of Department of Justice components, including arrangements related to law enforcement, exchange of information or counterlerrorism efforts as appropriate.

All Department of Justice components should continue to share Intelligence Information as appropriate within the U.S. Intelligence Community.

Appendix 8: REDRESS MOU

MEMORANDUM OF UNDERSTANDING
ON TERRORIST WATCHLIST REDRESS PROCEDURES

The Department of Justice (DOJ), the Federal Bureau of Investigation (FBI), the Terrorist Screening Center (TSC), the Department of Homeland Security (DHS), the Department of State (DOS), the Office of the Director of National Intelligence (ODNI), the National Counterterrorism Center (NCTC), the Central Intelligence Agency (CIA), the Department of Defense (DOD), and the Department of the Treasury (hereinafter referred to as the Parties);

Recognizing that the United States Government has developed a consolidated database of known and suspected terrorists that supports many different screening programs operated under distinct statutory and regulatory authorities;

Recognizing thai agencies that contribute to, compile, distribute, and use the consolidated database must use best efforts to maintain current, accurate, and thorough information;

Recognizing that the implementation of the screening programs nonetheless may, at times cause inconvenience, delay, or other adverse experiences for individuals during the terrorism screening process;

Recognizing that complaints received regarding the terrorism screening process should be expeditiously reviewed and addressed with dignity and respect;

Recognizing that the experience of travelers and other individuals interacting with government screening personnel is potentially affected by factors outside the terrorism screening scope of this Memorandum of Understanding, including, for example, random screening, screening for involvement with illicit drugs or other illegal conduct, behavioral screening criteria, as well as the basic professionalism and courtesy of government screening personnel, and that attention to these factors must be promoted through other appropriate means within the respective jurisdictions of the Parties;

Recognizing that on January 17, 2006, the Departments of State and Homeland Security announced an initiative on "Secure Borders and Open Doors in the Information Age," otherwise known as the Rice-Chertoff Initiative, including the establishment of a redress process to address perceived problems in international and domestic traveler screening; and

Having consulted with the Privacy and Civil Liberties Oversight Board and the privacy and civil liberties officials of DHS, DOL and ODNI, in developing the procedures contained in this agreement;

Hereby enter into this Memorandum of Undersianding (MOU).

1.   BACKGROUND

Homeland Security Presidential Directive 6 (HSPD)-6). "Integration and Use of Screening Information to Protect Against Terrorism," dated September 16, 2003, required the Attorney General to establish an organization to consolidate the Government's approach to terrorism screening and provide for the appropriate and lawful use of terrorist information in screening processes. Also on September 16. 2003. and in support of HSPD-6. the Memorandum of Understanding on the Integration and Use of Screening Information to Protect Against Terrorism (HSPD-6 MOU) was signed by the Secretary of State, the Attorney General, thee Secretary of Homeland Security, and the Director of Central Intelligence establishing TSC. On August 2, 2004, an addendum (Addendum A), which supplemented and incorporated by reference all provisions of the HSPD-6 MOU, was signed by the Secretary of the Treasury and the Secretary of Defense, in addition to the signatories of the HSPD-6 MOU. By their signatures on Addendum A, the Secretary of the Treasury and the Secretary of Defense also became signatories to the HSPD-6 MOU. In 2007, Addendum A was superseded by Addendum B, which added the Director of National Intelligence and the Director of the TSC as signatories.

2.   PURPOSE, SCOPE, AND CONSTRUCTION

The purpose of this MOU is to set forth the mutual understanding of the Parties to establish and implement a coordinated redress process to respond to individual complaints about adverse experiences during terrorism screening that relate to the use of information contained in the government's consolidated database of known and suspected terrorists, known as the Terrorist Screening Database or TSDB This MOU is intended to complement, and shall not be construed to conflict with the Constitution, statutes, or regulations of the United States or any Party's legal authority to process screening-related complaints or appeals, to the extent that any provision of this MOU conflicts with any Party's legal authority for screening or to hear appeals, the conflicting provisions of this MOU shall not apply. This MOU does not apply to individual complaints, or parts thereof, that pertain to screening experiences that are unrelated to the use of information contained in the TSDB.

Any reference in this MOU to a Party or Parties shall also be understood to refer to any components of such Party or Parties to the extent that such components fall within the definition of screening agency or nominating/originating agency as set forth below, or that such components have been designated by the Party or Parties as having obligations arising from this MOU. Nothing in this MOU precludes any Party from conducting periodic reviews of individuals in the TSDB to determine whether an individual should remain in the TSDB, have their TSDB status modified, or be removed from the TSDB. Nothing in this MOU shall be construed to interfere with, limit, or impede any Party's ability to protect information that is classified pursuant to Executive Order 12958, as amended, or is otherwise protected by law from disclosure.

3.   DEFINITIONS

As used in this MOU, these terms or phrases are defined as follows:

   A) *Complaint or Redress Complaint:* An individual's statement about an allegedly adverse experience or outcome during a terrorism screening process, which usually includes a request for assistance or a remedy.
   B) *Derogatory Information:* The information relied upon or generated by a nominating/originating agency to support the nomination of an individual to the TSDB.
   C) *Known or Suspected Terrorist:* As defined by HSPD-6, an individual known or appropriately suspected to be or to have been engaged in conduct constituting, in preparation for, in aid of, or related to terrorism. Pursuant to HSPD-6, the TSDB shall include identifying information about all known or suspected terrorists.
   D) *Misidentified Person:* An individual who has had an adverse experience or outcome during

terrorism screening because the individual is a near match to a known or suspected terrorist in the TSDB. Misidentified persons are not actually listed in the TSDB but usually share an identical or very similar name and date of birth with a person in the TSDB, which causes them to be delayed or otherwise inconvenienced during screening.

E) *Nominating Agency:* A Federal agency that has determined that an individual is a known or suspected terrorist and nominates that individual to the TSDB based on information that originated with that agency and/or a third agency.

F) *Originating Agency:* A Federal agency that generates derogatory or identifying information about a known or suspected terrorist.

G) *Personally Identifiable Information:* Any representation of information that permits the identity of an individual to whom the information applies to be reasonably inferred by either direct or indirect means including any other information, which is linked to such individual.

H) *Redress:* The process whereby an individual may seek the help of a screening agency in addressing the cause of an adverse experience or outcome related to the use of TSDB data by filing a complaint with the screening agency. The screening agency or its designee, in cooperation with TSC and the nominating/originating agency, provides assistance by determining the cause of that adverse experience, verifying that all relevant information relied upon in the screening process is thorough, accurate, and current, and making any warranted corrections to pertinent records. The redress process as defined in this paragraph does not apply to complaints related to the visa application process.

I) *Screening Agency:* Any agency that conducts terrorism screening. A screening agency acquires information for the purpose of determining whether an individual is a known or suspected terrorist in the TSDB, and evaluates and/or uses that information in order to take a particular governmental action with respect to an individual, such as requiring additional physical security screening at an airport security checkpoint, determining admissibility into the United Stales, or similar governmental action. The DOS and DHS shall not be considered screening agencies with respect to the visa application process.

J) *Terrorism Screening:* The evaluation of an individual to determine whether he or she is a known or suspected terrorist identified in the TSDB in order to take a particular governmental action with respect to an individual, such as requiring additional physical security screening at an airport security checkpoint, determining admissibility into the United States, or similar governmental action.

K) *Terrorist Screening Database or TSDB:* The Federal government's consolidated database that contains identifying information about known or suspected terrorists. It is also commonly known as the consolidated terrorist watchlist. The TSDB is a sensitive but unclassified database and does not contain any derogatory information.

L) *TIDE:* NC'TC's Terrorist Identities Datamart Environment (TIDE), which is a classified database containing the derogatory information that supports the nominations of known or suspected international terrorists to the TSDB.

4. <u>RESPONSIBILITIES OF THE PARTIES</u>

A) <u>Responsibilities of All Parties:</u>
   i. <u>Designation of Responsible Official.</u> Each Party will identify a senior official who will be responsible for ensuring the Parly's full participation in the redress process and overall compliance with this MOU. A Party may also designate redress officials for components of that Party that perform screening or nominating/originating agency functions. The Parties agree to identify these officials and exchange the names of these officials no later than 30 calendar days after this MOU becomes effective and update the information as needed

thereafter.

ii. <u>Resources.</u> Subject to the availability of funds, each Party will identify and commit appropriate staff and other resources to carry out responsibilities under this MOU. This includes identifying the office(s) responsible for carrying out the Party's responsibilities pertaining to the processing of individual redress complaints as set forth in this MOU. The Parties agree to exchange the names and contact information for the responsible offices no later than 30 calendar dnys after this MOU becomes effective, and update the information as needed thereafter.

iii. <u>Information Sharing.</u> Each Party will share all information relevant to the resolution of a complaint with other Parties to the extent necessary to carry out this MOU or to defend any judicial challenge to the resolution of a complaint, consistent with legal requirements and classification and handling controls. A Party may provide the relevant information in a summarized or substituted format to protect sensitive sources and methods.

iv. <u>Protection of Personally Identifiable Information.</u> Each Party will take appropriate action to proleel personally identifiable information (Pll) in its own record systems related to a redress matter against unauthorized access and to ensure that PII is handled in a way that provides security and accountability. When Parties transmit Pll related to a redress matter via non-electronic or electronic means, such as email, facsimile, portable media or otherwise, the Parties will properly mark the data and/or comnuinications/media/device to provide appropriate notice of the existence of PII and will ensure the means of transmission are secured by encryption or equivalent protections.

v. <u>Administrative Record.</u> Each Party will be responsible for maintaining the administrative records necessary to document its participation in the redress process.

vi. <u>Updating Agency Records.</u> Each Party that maintains data related to the terrorist watchlist in its paper and/or electronic recordkeeping systems will update its records (i.e.. correct, modify, or delete) expeditiously once notified of a change to an individual's watchlist status as the result of the disposition of a redress matter. This provision applies to data in government information systems (e.g.. TIDE., Treasury Enforcement Communications System/Interagency Border Inspection System (TECS/IBIS), No-Fly List, Consular Lookout And Support System) used for watchlist creation or screening purposes. It is not intended to require the Parties to change records that reflect actions already taken based on watchlist status, unless and only to the extent that the record will have an unwarranted adverse impact on the individual seeking redress.

vii. <u>Litigation.</u> Subject to paragraph 4.A.iii above, each Party agrees to cooperate with DOJ to assist in defending any judicial challenge to the resolution of a redress complaint processed under this MOU or a determination by a screening agency that relied in whole or in part on records or information in the TSDB. This provision shall not be construed to limit DOS's discretion under section 222(I) of the Immigration and Nationality Act (INA), 8 U.S.C.§ 1202(f), concerning the disclosure of visa records in litigation.

viii. <u>Privacy Act Compliance.</u> In carrying out this MOU, each Party is responsible for its own compliance with the Privacy Act of 1974, 5 U.S.C. §§ 552a *et seq.*, in the collection, maintenance, use. And dissemination of personally identifiable information. Within 30 calendar days after the effective date of this MOU, each Party agrees to review its applicable Privacy Act system of records notices and any relevant forms used to collect information from the public where such information may ultimately be used during the redress process. Each Parly agrees to make appropriate changes to those documents, if necessary, including the publication of new or modified routine uses to permit the sharing of information to resolve redress matters and related litigation.

ix. <u>Record Retention.</u> Each Party agrees to retain its redress records for at least six years from the date of final agency disposition. Agencies may elect to establish a longer retention period to meet statutory, regulatory, or operational requirements.

x. <u>Requests for Disclosure of TSDB Data.</u> Unless and until TSC advises the Parties of an alternate procedure, each Party agrees that it will contact TSC's legal counsel if it receives a request for information or records that it knows would reveal an individual's status (positive or negative) in the TSDB or would otherwise reveal the contents of TSDB data. TSC legal counsel will provide timely guidance on how to respond to these requests. This provision also pertains to requests for TSDB data resident in supported screening systems, such as the No-fly list, TECS/ IBIS, the National Crime Information Center's Violent Gang and Terrorist Organization File (VGTOF). and the DOS's Consular Lookout and Support System (CLASS).

B) <u>Responsibilities of Screening Agencies:</u>

i. <u>Designation of Responsibilities.</u> Any Party that is a screening agency may designate another Party, with the other Party's consent if needed, to perform the responsibilities outlined in section 4.B. of this MOU. In addition, where a screening agency is a component of a Party, the Party may determine at its discretion that any responsibility of that screening agency may be performed in whole or in part by the Party.

ii. <u>Resources.</u> Subject to the availability of funds, each screening agency will designate or create an office to carry out its operational responsibilities for redress. Where a Party has several components that perform terrorism screening, the responsible official for that Party (see Section 4.A.i above) will determine whether a single centralized office or separate offices in the appropriate components, or some combination of the two. will perform this function. Subject to the availability of funds, each screening agency will commit sufficient and appropriate staff and resources to that office or offices to ensure redress complaints are processed in a timely and efficient manner. The screening agencies agree to notify the other Parties of the identity of and contact information for the designated offices under this paragraph no later than 30 calendar days after this MOU becomes effective and update that information as needed.

iii. <u>Receipt and Initial Processing of Complaints.</u> Each screening agency will have a procedure for receiving complaints from members of the public. If the screening agency receives a complaint from an individual who appears to be in the TSDB and the complaint relates to an adverse effect in the screening process arising out of his her placement in the TSDB, the agency will forward a copy of the complaint and related information to TSC within a reasonable time. The screening agency will be responsible for verifying the identity of the complainant in accordance with the screening agency's applicable regulations and policies. When forwarding a complaint to TSC, the screening agency must provide: (1) all relevant correspondence from the individual. (2) copies of any relevant internal agency records, and (3) information identifying the complainant including, at a minimum, the complainant's full name, date of birth, and place of citizenship. After consultation with affected Parties, TSC may revise these requirements in the future as needed for expeditious processing of redress complaints. No amendment to the MOU would be required to effectuate such a change.

iv. <u>Follow-up with the Complainant.</u> If requested by TSC, the screening agency will contact the complainant to request additional information to assist TSC or the nominating/originating agency in verifying the complainant's identity and processing the complaint. Nothing in this subsection precludes a screening agency from contacting the complainant in accordance with the screening agency's procedures or discretion.

v. <u>Response to the Complainant.</u> Screening agencies are responsible for providing a written response to complaints they receive based on information provided by TSC and the nominating/originating agency. Because of the sensitivity of the TSDB and derogatory information, the content of any response to a complaint must be coordinated with TSC and the nominating/originating agency through TSC. Screening agencies may use standardized response letters that have been coordinated in advance In the screening agency, TSC, and DOJ.

    vi. <u>Redress for Misidentilied Persons.</u> On January 17, 2006,DHS and DOS announced an initiative on "Secure Borders and Open Doors in the Information Age," otherwise known as the Rice-Chertoff Initiative, which includes the establishment of a redress process to address perceived problems in international and domestic traveler screening. The DHS Screening Coordination Office is leading the inter-agency effort to fulfill the goals of the Rice-Chertoff Initiative, which is intended to improve the redress process for persons who are misidentilied during traveler screening processes, among other improvements

    vii. <u>Administrative Appeals.</u> If the screening agency has established an administrative appeals process for redress determinations or other agency determinations in which the TSDB was used, the screening agency will notify TSC after receiving any such administrative appeal and work with TSC, as needed, to process the appeal, and coordinate the final agency response with TSC. The screening agency will provide all relevant paperwork to TSC (including a copy of the appeal letter and any information submitted by the individual on their own behalf). When the screening agency has the legal authority to make the final decision on the appeal, it will promptly notify TSC of that decision.

    viii.   <u>Litigation.</u> When the screening agency becomes aware of litigation arising out of terrorism screening, the screening agency will notify TSC and DOJ as soon as possible after identifying the nexus to the TSDB. Notification should occur as soon as the Party learns of an individual's intent to sue or immediately after being served with legal process.

C) <u>Responsibilities of the Terrorist Screening Center:</u>
    i. <u>Receipt and Coordination of Complaints.</u> TSC will receive complaints from screening agencies

    ii. and research them to determine the nature and cause of the individual's adverse experience. TSC will track all complaints and will be responsible for facilitating any inter-agency coordination necessary to properly research the complaint and respond to the screening agency regarding the outcome (e.g., any corrections made or recommended).

    iii. <u>Review of Basis for Inclusion in the TSDB.</u> In cases where the complainant is or appears to be in the TSDB. TSC will provide copies of the complaint letter and other relevant information to NCTC and/or the nominating/originating agency to assist in the resolution of the complaint TSC will then work with NCTC and/or the nominating/originating agency, as appropriate, to determine whether the complainant's current status in the TSDB is appropriate based on the most current, accurate, and thorough information available. TSC may ask NCTC and/or the nominating/originating agency to provide updated information or analysis to assist in this determination as well as for a recommendation on addressing the complaint.

    iv. <u>Determination.</u> Alter reviewing the available information and considering any recommendation from the nominating/originating agency. TSC will make a determination whether the record should remain in the TSDB, have its TSDB status modified, or be removed, unless the legal authority to make such a determination resides, in whole or in part, with another agency. In such cases, TSC will only prepare a recommendation for the decision-making agency and will implement any determination once made. TSC will take any necessary action to implement the determination, such as removing the record from the

TSDB or modifying the record's status in the TSDB (e.g., downgrade from No-Fly to Selectee). Before taking action that is inconsistent with a recommendation of the nominating/originating agency. TSC will notify NCTC, which will convey that determination back to the nonimanating/originating agency, unless the nominating/originating agency is the FBI, in which case TSC will contact the FBI directly. The nominating/originating agency will then be responsible for addressing the conflict with TSC or the decision-making agency either directly or through NCTC. The Parties will then coordinate on an agreed-to resolution.

v. <u>Update of the TSDB.</u> TSC will ensure that TSDB records are appropriately deleted or modified in accordance with a determination on a redress matter. TSC will also verify that such removals or modifications carry over to other screening systems that receive TSDB data (e.g., TECS/IBIS, No-Fly list).

vi. <u>Deconfliction.</u> In the event of a multi-agency nomination where the nominating and/or originating agencies do not agree on what recommendation should be made on a specific redress matter. TSC will request that the agencies consult with one another and share appropriate information about the watchlisted individual in an attempt to prov ide a joint recommendation to TSC. If the nominating/originating agencies cannot agree to a joint recommendation. TSC (or other agency with the legal authority to make the decision) will make the final determination considering the information provided by each agency.

vii. <u>Review Related to Misidentified Persons.</u> If a complainant's adverse experience or outcome during terrorism screening is a result of being a near match ("misidentified") to a record in the TSDB, and that complaint is referred to TSC by the screening agency, TSC will review the record in the TSDB, as described in the paragraphs above, to ensure the TSDB record is valid and satisfies the criteria for inclusion in the TSDB and determine if additional information can be added to TIDE, the TSDB, or other agency systems to reduce the likelihood of a future misidentification. If the record does not meet the criteria, it will be removed from the TSDB.

viii. <u>Administrative Appeals.</u> TSC will work with a screening agency to assist it in processing any administrative appeal of a redress determination or other determination in which the TSDB was used. When TSC receives notice of an appeal, TSC will notify NCTC and/or the nominating/originating agency as soon as possible. TSC will facilitate communications between the nominating/originating and screening agencies on the following issues: (1) determining what material may be releasable to the individual during appeal (if applicable), and (2) updating the analysis of any information that may have developed since the original determination and/or any information that was provided by the individual on his or her behalf during the appeals process itself. After reviewing the available information and considering any recommendation from the nominating/originating agency, TSC will make a determination whether the record should remain in the TSDB, have its TSDB status modified, or be removed, unless the legal authority to make such a determination resides, in whole or in part, with another agency. In such cases. TSC will only prepare a recommendation for the decision-making agency and will implement any determination once made.

ix. <u>Litigation.</u> When TSC becomes aware of litigation arising out of terrorism screening. TSC will notify NCTC, the nominating/originating agency, and DOJ as soon as possible.

D) <u>Responsibilities of the National Counterterrorism Center:</u>
   i. <u>Review, Coordination, and Research of Complaints.</u> Upon receipt of a complaint from TSC. NCTC will review its holdings, notify the nominating/originating agency of the complaint, and provide the nominating/originating agency with a copy of the complaint for review.

NCTC will then request that the nominating/originating agency and, as appropriate, any other agency with relevant information, review their holdings and provide NCTC information relevant to the complaint. This may include updated information or analysis regarding the complainant's current status in the TSDB. derogatory information, identifying information that might he relevant to a misidentification, or other potentially relevant information or analysis (including that which lends to show that the individual is not a known or suspected terrorist, or which otherwise tends to cast doubt on the derogatory information). NCTC will also request that the nominating/originating agency provide its recommendation regarding resolution of the complaint. With the concurrence of the nominating/originating agency, NCTC will provide that agency's recommendation and any other relevant information to TSC. Should TSC or another agency disagree with the recommendation. NCTC will assist in the deconfliction process as set forth above. NCTC generally will not receive or process complaints or appeals for individuals nominated only by the FBI.

ii. Review Related to Misidentified Persons. If a complainant's adverse experience or outcome during terrorism screening was the result of being a near match ("misidentified") to a record in the TSDB. and that complaint is referred to TSC by the screening agency, NCTC will work with TSC and the nominating/originating agency to ensure the TSDB record is valid and satisfies the criteria for inclusion in the TSDB, and determine if additional information can be added to TIDE, the TSDB, or other agency systems to reduce the likelihood of a future misidentification.

iii. Update of TIDE. NCTC will promptly update TIDE records with any new derogatory or other relevant information (including that which tends to show that the individual is not a known or suspected terrorist, or which otherwise lends to cast doubt on the derogatory information) pertaining to individuals in the TSDB. NCTC will also modify TIDE in a timely fashion to reflect modifications to TSDB nominations resulting from a redress complaint and will make appropriate changes to a given TIDE record when it is necessary to trigger electronically conforming changes to the TSDB record.

iv. Administrative Appeals. NCTC will work with TSC. as needed, to assist it in processing any administrative appeal of a redress determination or other determination in which the TSDB was used, including coordinating communication between TSC, the screening agency, and the relevant nominating/originating agency, as necessary. NCTC's primary role will be to coordinate administrative appeal requests by TSC with the appropriate nominating/originating agency in the Intelligence Community other than the FBI.

E) Responsibilities of Nominating/Originating Agencies:
   i. Review, Coordination, and Research of Complaints. Once notified of a redress complaint by TSC or NCTC, the nominating/originating agency will review the derogatory information that is the basis for including the complainant in the TSDB. In coordination with NCTC, when appropriate, the nomimiting/originating agency w ill evaluate whether the complainant continues to satisfy the criteria for inclusion in the TSDB, as well as any other relevant criteria, such as those for the No-Fly and Selectee Lists. The nominating/originating agency will determine whether updated information or analysis exists, including information from other agencies, and incorporate any such information in its response. The nominating/originating agency will also consider any information provided through the redress process by the individual, the screening agency, NCTC, or TSC. The nominating/originating agency shall take appropriate steps to modify, correct, or delete its holdings to reflect any changes made to TIDE as a result of the redress process, or that otherwise have been determined to be in error as a result of the redress process.

ii. Recommendation. The nominating/originating agency may make a recommendalion to TSC as to the resolution of any complaint. Continued inclusion in the TSDB must be supported by derogatory information in TIDE. When the nominating/originating agency has additional derogatory or other relevant information that is not in TIDE, the nominating/originating agency will ensure that NCTC and TSC are notified, and will work with NCTC and TSC to ensure that such information is added to TIDE in a manner that provides meaningful information while protecting sources and methods. Every effort should be made, however, to share the derogatory information with TSC whenever possible.

iii. Deconfliction. In the event of a multi-agency nomination where the nominating and/or originating agencies do not agree on what rccommcndalion should be made on a specific redress matter, the agencies will consult with one another at TSC's request and share appropriate information about the watchlisted individual in an attempt to provide a joint recommendation to TSC. If the nominating/originating agencies cannot agree to a joint recommendation. TSC will make the final determination considering all of the available information.

iv. Review Related to Misidentified Persons. If a complainant's adverse experience during terrorism screening was the result of being a near match ("misidentified") to a record in the TSDB, the nominating/originating agency of that record will work with TSC and NCTC, as appropriate, to ensure the TSDB record is valid and satisfies the criteria for inclusion in the TSDB, and if additional information can be added to TIDE, the TSDB, or other agency systems to reduce the likelihood of a future misidentification.

v. Administrative Appeals. Each nominating/originating agency will work with TSC and NCTC, as needed, to assist them in processing an appeal of a redress determination or other determination in which the TSDB was used. The nominating/originating agency will be responsible for advising the screening agency on the releasability of any materials requested by an appellant during an appeal. An updated analysis of all relevant information will he coordinated between NCTC, and the nominating/originating agency, and will be forwarded to TSC, which in turn will provide it to the screening agency. The analysis will consider any new information developed since the initial determination, as well as any information provided by the individual on his or her own behalf during the appeals process itself.

F) Responsibilities of the Department of Justice:
   i. DOJ will coordinate with the relevant Parties during the defense of any judicial challenge to the resolution of a complaint processed under this MOU or a determination by a screening agency that relied in whole or in part on records or information in the TSDB.
   ii. DOJ will consult with the Parties, as necessary, to provide continuing legal advice and support on matters related to watchlisting redress and this MOU.

G) Visa Application Process, DOS and DHS Responsibilities at the Time of Visa Refusal:
   i. DOS and DHS will continue to comply with applicable visa procedures, which may include an at-post internal review by a supervisory consular officer or another appropriate official. While a consular officer's denial of a visa application may not be overruled, that determination is informed by an internal management review and, in appropriate cases, by input from an interagency review.
   ii. If a visa application is refused, applicants are advised that they may re-apply for a visa. A subsequent application is considered as a new case. DOS agrees to continue to review the underlying data and facts in such subsequent applications. Whenever appropriate, DOS consults with TSC, NCTC, and other agencies regarding data that appears incomplete or inaccurate, or otherwise conflicts with information obtained in the visa application process.

5. SETTLEMENT OF DISPUTES

Except as set forth in paragraphs 4.C.v and 4.E.iii concerning the deconfliction of watchlist nominations, disagreements between the Parties arising under or related to this MOU will be resolved only by consultation between the Parties.

6. OTHER PROVISIONS.

This MOU is not intended to conflict with either the Constitution or current federal statutes, regulations, or the directives of the Parties. If any term or provision of this MOU is inconsistent with such authority, then the term or provision shall be inapplicable to that Parly and any other Party that is dependent upon the first Parly's action to perform its responsibilities, but the remaining terms and conditions of this MOU shall continue to apply.

7. AMENDMENT

This MOU may be amended at any time by the mutual written consent of the Parties' authorized representatives. Modification within the scope of this MOU shall be made by the issuance of a fully executed addendum prior to any changes in responsibilities being performed.

8. TERMINATION

The terms of this MOU, as it may be amended, will remain in effect indefinitely. To terminate its participation in this MOU, a Party must give at least 30 days prior written notice. In the event of termination, each Party will continue with full participation up to the effective date of termination.

9. NO OBLIGATION of FUNDS

This MOU does not constitute an obligation to expend funds by any Party. Unless otherwise agreed in writing, each Party shall bear any costs it incurs in relation to this MOU. Expenditures will be subject to federal budgetary processes and availability of funds pursuant to applicable laws and regulations. The Parlies expressly acknowledge that this MOU in no way implies that Congress will appropriate funds for such expenditures.

10. NO PRIVATE RIGHTS

This MOU is an internal arrangement between the Parties and is not intended, and should not be construed, to create any right or benefit, substantive or procedural, enforceable at law or otherwise by any third party against the Parties, their parent or component agencies, the United States, or the officers, employees, agents or other associated personnel thereof.

11. EFFECTIVE DATE

The terms of this MOU will become effective on the date on which it is signed by all Parties The MOU may be signed in counterparts.

12. PERIODIC REVIEW

The Responsible Officials designated by the Parties pursuant to section 4 A.i will meet on an annual basis or at the request of any Party to discuss and review the implementation of this MOU. Failure of the parties to conduct annual reviews will not result in the termination of activities provided for under this MOU.

13.   POINTS OF CONTACT

Points of contact (POCs) for the Parties, identified below, are responsible for identifying the responsible officials and redress resources pursuant to sections 4.A.i and ii, and 4.B.ii and providing that information to the other POCs.

A) The POC for the Department of Justice will be the Chief Privacy and Civil Liberties Officer.
B) The POC for the Federal Bureau of Investigation will be the Section Chief of the National Threat Center Section, Counterterrorism Division.
C) The POC for the Terrorist Screening Center will be the Privacy Officer.
D) The POC for the National Counterterrorism Center will be the Chief of the Terrorist Identities Group.
E) The POC for the Department of Homeland Security will be the Director of the Screening Coordination Office.
F) The POC for the Department of State will be the Director of Information Management and Liaison Staff, Visa Office.
G) The POC for the Office of the Director of National Intelligence will be the Civil Liberties Protection Officer.
H) The POC for the Central Intelligence Agency will be the Chief of Policy and Community Action Staff(PCAS).
I) The POC for the Department of Defense will be the Director, Joint Intelligence Task Force for Combating Terrorism, Defense Intelligence Agency.
J) The POC for the Department of the Treasury will be the Assistant General Counsel (Enforcement and Intelligence).

The foregoing represents the understanding reached by the Parties.

APPROVED BY:

Condoleezza Rice   Date
Secretary of State

Henry VI. Paulson, Jr.   Date
Secrctary of the Treasury

Alberto R. Gonzales   Date
Attorney General

Robert M. Gates   Date
Secretary of Defense

Michael Chertoff   Date
Secrctary of Homeland Security

John D. Negroponte   Date
Director of National Intelligence

Robert S. Mueller, III   Date
Director, Federal Bureau of Investigation

John Scott Redd   Date
Director, National Counterterrorism Center

Gen. Michael V. Hayden   Date
Director, Central Intelligence Agency

Richard S. Kopel   Date
Acting Director, Terrorist Screening Center

Appendix 9: PRESIDENTIAL MEMORANDUM REGARDING 12/25/2009 TERRORIST ATTACK

January 7, 2010

MEMORANDUM FOR   THE SECRETARY OF STATE
                                  THE SECRETARY OF DEFENSE
                                  THE ATTORNEY GENERAL
                                  THE SECRETARY ENERGY
                                  THE SECRETARY OF HOMELAND SECURITY
                                  THE DIRECTOR OF NATIONAL INTELLIGENCE
                                  THE DIRECTOR OF THE CENTRAL INTELLIGENCE AGENCY
                                  THE DIRECTOR OF THE FEDERAL BUREAU OF INVESTIGATION
                                  THE DIRECTOR OF THE NATIONAL SECURITY AGENCY
                                  THE DIRECTOR OF THE NATIONAL COUNTERTERRORISM
                                           CENTER

SUBJECT: Attempted Terrorist Attack on December 25. 2009: Intelligence, Screening, and Watchlisting System Corrective Actions

After receiving the conclusions of the White House-led review of the U.S. watchlisting system and the performance of the intelligence, homeland security, and law enforcement communities as related to the attempt to bring down a Detroit-bound flight on December 25 by detonating an explosive device, and a Department of Homeland Security-led review on Aviation Screening, Technology and Procedures; I have concluded that immediate actions must be taken to enhance the security of the American people. These actions are necessary given inherent systemic weaknesses and human errors revealed by the review of events leading up to December 25th. They also are required to ensure that the standards, practices, and business processes that have been in place since the aftermath of 9/11 are appropriately robust to address the evolving terrorist threat facing our Nation in the coming years.

Department of State
- Review visa issuance and revocation criteria and processes, with special emphasis on counterterrorism concerns: determine how technology enhancements can facilitate and strengthen visa-related business processes.

Department of Homeland Security
- Aggressively pursue enhanced screening technology, protocols, and procedures, especially in regard to aviation and other transportation sectors, consistent with privacy rights and civil liberties; strengthen international partnerships and coordination on aviation security issues.
- Develop recommendations on long-term law enforcement requirements for aviation security in coordination with the Department of Justice.

Director of National Intelligence
- Immediately reaffirm and clarify roles and responsibilities of the counterterrorism analytic components of the Intelligence Community in synchronizing, correlating, and analyzing all sources of intelligence related to terrorism.
- Accelerate information technology enhancements, to include knowledge discovery, database

integration, cross-database searches, and the ability to correlate biographic information with terrorism-related intelligence.

- Take further steps to enhance the rigor and raise the standard of tradecraft of intelligence analysis, especially analysis designed to uncover and prevent terrorist plots.
- Ensure resources are properly aligned with issues highlighted in strategic warning analysis.

The Central Intelligence Agcncy

- Issue guidance aimed at ensuring the timely distribution of intelligence reports
- Strengthen procedures related to how watchlisting information is entered, reviewed, searched, analyzed, and acted upon

Federal Bureau of Investigation/Terrorist Screening Center

- Conduct a thorough review of Terrorist Screening Database holdings and ascertain current visa status of all "known and suspected terrorists." beginning with the No Fly list.
- Develop recommendations on whether adjustments are needed to the Watchlisting Nominations Guidance, including biographic and derogatory criteria for inclusion in the Terrorist Identities Datamart Environment and Terrorist Screening Database, as well as the subset Selectee and No Fly lists.

National Counterterrorism Center

- Establish and resource appropriately a process to prioritize and to pursue thoroughly and exhaustively terrorism threat threads, to include the identification of appropriate follow-up action by the intelligence, law enforcement, and homeland security communities.
- Establish a dedicated capability responsible for enhancing record information on possible terrorists in the Terrorist Identities Datamart Environment for watchlisting purposes.

National Security Agency

- Develop and begin implementation of a training course to enhance analysts' awareness of watchlisting processes and procedures in partnership with National Counterterrorism Terrorist Center and the Terrorist Screening Center.

National Security Staff

- Initiate an interagency policy process to review the systemic failures leading to the attempted terror attack on December 25. 2009, in order to make needed policy adjustments and to clarify roles and responsibilities within the counterterrorism community.
- Initiate an interagency review of the watchlisting process, including business processes, procedures, and criteria for watchlisting, and the interoperability and sufficiency of supporting information technology systems.

I have designated my Assistant for Homeland Security and Counterterrorism John Brennan to be the responsible and accountable White House official to ensure rapid progress is made in all areas. A monthly status report on actions underway should be submitted to me through Mr. Brennan. In addition, I am directing Mr. Brennan to work with departments and agencies and the Office of Management and Budget on resource requirements that are neccssary to address the shortcomings uncovered by our review. Finally, I will ask my Intelligence Advisory Board to look at broader analytic and intelligence issues associated with this incident, including how to meet the challenge associated with exploiting the ever-increasing volume of information available to the Intelligence Community. As we go forward, it is imperative that we work together to correct problems highlighted by this incident, focusing on concrete solutions. We are all responsible for the safety and security of the American people and must redouble our efforts to be effective in carrying out this solemn responsibility.

//Signed//
Barack Obama

Appendix 10: ACRONYMS AND ABBREVIATIONS

Acronym	Description
Addendum B	Addendum B to the Memorandum of Understanding on the Integration and Use of Screening Information to Protect Against Terrorism, Signed by The Secretary of State, the Secretary of the Treasury, the Secretary of Defense, the Attorney General, the Secretary of Homeland Security, the Director of National Intelligence, the Director of the Central Intelligence Agency, the Director of the National Counterterrorism Center, the Director of the Terrorist Screening Center
A-File	Alien Registration File (DHS)
AIS	Automated Identification System
ALA	Airport Liaison Agents and Attaches (FBI)
API	Advanced Passenger Information
ATM	Automated Teller Machine
ATS	Automated Targeting System (DHS)
CBP	U.S. Customs and Border Protection (DHS)
CBRN	Chemical, Biological, Radiological, or Nuclear
CCD	Consular Consolidated Database (DOS)
CIA	Central Intelligence Agency
CJIS	Criminal Justice Information Services Division (FBI)
CLASS	Consular Lookout And Support System (DOS)
CTD	Counterterrorism Division (FBI)
DC	Deputies Committee
DC I	Director of Central Intelligence (now the DNI)
DHS	Department of Homeland Security
DIA	Defense Intelligence Agency (DoD)
DoD	Department of Defense
DOJ	Department of Justice
DOMEX	Document and Media Exploitation
DOS	Department of State
DSR	Daily Summary Reports (TSC)
DTO	Designated Terrorist Organization
EFPs	Explosively Formed Projectiles/Penetrators
EMA	Encounter Management Application (TSC)
ERO	Enforcement and Removal Operations (DHS/ICE)
ESEL	Expanded Selectee List

ESTA	Electronic System for Travel Authorization
FBI	Federal Bureau of Investigation
FIN	Fingerprint Identification Number (DHS)
FISA	Foreign Intelligence Surveillance Act
FGI	Foreign Government Information
FTO	Foreign Terrorist Organization
FTTTF	Foreign Terrorist Tracking Task Force (FBI)
HAZMAT	Hazardous Materials
HSPD-11	Homeland Security Presidential Directive - 11, Comprehensive Terrorist-Related Screening Procedures
HSPD-24	Homeland Security Presidential Directive-24, Biometrics for Identification and Screening to Enhancc National Security
HSPD-6	Homeland Security Presidential Directive-6, Integration and Use of Screening Information to Protect Against Terrorism
I&A	Office of Intelligence & Analysis (DHS)
IAFIS	Integrated Automatic Fingerprint Identification System (FBI/CJIS)
IAP	Immigration Advisory Program
ICE	U.S. Immigration and Customs Enforcement (DHS)
IED	Improvised Explosive Device
IIR	Intelligence Information Report
INA	Immigration and Nationality Act
Information Sharing MOU	Memorandum of Understanding between the Intelligence Community, Federal Law Enforcement Agencies, and the Department of Homeland Security Concerning Information Sharing, dated March 4, 2003
IP	Internet Protocol
IPC	Interagency Policy Committee (IPC) is an interagency group led by the White House National Security Staff to establish Administration policies
IRPTA	Intelligence Reform and Prevention Act
ISA	The Information Sharing and Access Interagency Policy Committee (ISA IPC) is the While House led group that specifically addresses watchlisting policies for the U.S. Government
ISE	Information Sharing Environment
JTTF	Joint Terrorist Task Force
JWICS	Joint Worldwide Intelligence Communications System
KSTF	Known or Suspected Terrorist File (Federal Bureau of Investigation, National Crime Information Center, formerly Violent Gang and Terrorist Organization File (VGTOF)
LEGAT	Legal Attachés (FBI)

LEO	Law Enforcement Online
LPR	Lawful Permanent Resident
MOU	Memorandum of Understanding
NCIC	National Crime Information Center (FBI)
NCTC	National Counterterrorism Center
NDIU	Nominations and Data Integrity Unit (TSC)
NICS	National Instant Criminal Background Check System
NIPF	National Intelligence Priorities Framework
NIPF-CT	National Intelligence Priorities Framework - Counterterrorism
NIV	Non-Immigrant Visa
NMEC	National Media Exploitation Center
NORTHCOM	Northern Command (DoD)
NTC-C	National Targeting Center-Cargo (DHS/CBP)
NTC-P	National Targeting Center - Passenger (DHS/CBP)
NVMC	National Vessel Movement Center (DHS)
OIA	Office of Intelligence and Analysis (DHS/TSA)
OTW	One Time Waiver
PIERS	Passport Information Electronic Records System
PNR	Passenger Name Records
POE	Port of Entry
RDD	Radioactive/Radiation Dispersal Device
Redress MOU	Memorandum of Understanding on Terrorist Watchlist Redress Procedures
SDGT	Specially Designated Global Terrorist
SDT	Specially Designated Terrorist
SIPRNET	Secret Internet Protocol Router Network
SME	Subjcct Matter Expert
SDNL	Specially Designated Nationals List
SRQ	Single Review Queue (TSC)
TACTICS	TipofT Australia Counterterrorism information Control System
TBU	Threat-based expedited upgrade
TECS	*No longer an acronym.* Previously Treasury Enforcement Communications System.
TIDE	Terrorist Identities Datamart Environment
TIPOFF	*Not an acronym. Also seen as Tipoff.*
TREX	Terrorist Review and Examination Unit (TSC)
TRIP	Traveler Redress Inquiry Program (DHS)

TSA	Transportation Security Administration (DHS)
TSC	Terrorist Screening Center
TSC MOU	Memorandum of Understanding on the Integration and Use of Screening Information to Protect Against Terrorism
TSDB	Terrorist Screening Database
TSOC	Terrorist Screening Operations Center *(formerly Terrorist Screening Tactical Operations Center (TSTOC))*(TSC)
TSOU	Terrorist Screening Operations Unit (TSC)
TTIC	Terrorist Threat Integration Center (now NCTC)
TUSCAN	Tipoff United States Canada
TWIC	Transportation Worker Identification Credential (DHS/TSA)
U.S.	United States
U//FOUO	Unclassified, for official use only
UNSCR	United Nations Security Council Resolution
URL	Uniform Resource Locator
USAID	United States Agency for International Development
USCG	United States Coast Guard (DHS)
USCIS	U.S. Citizenship and Immigration Services (DHS)
USSS	United States Secret Service (DHS)
VIN	Vehicle Identification Number
WLS	Watchlist Service (DHS)

Appendix 11 SUMMARY OF CHANGES AND UPDATES FROM THE 2010 WATCHLISTING GUIDANCE

Summary of Changes and Updates from the 2010 Watchlisting Guidance

The Watchlisting Guidance is a comprehensive document detailing the U.S. Government's terrorist watchlisting policies and procedures. It was originally developed to help standardize the watchlisting community's nomination and screening processes. Since approval of the Watchlisting Guidance in July of 2010, the guidance and its related appendices have undergone a thorough interagency review as a result of a May 2010 Deputy's Committee tasking to the White House National Security Staff Information Sharing and Access Interagency Policy Committee (IPC) that any significant issues or required changes be brought back to the Deputies for discussion. The Information Sharing and Access IPC identified a number of changes in Department and Agency watchlisting practices that had evolved since dissemination of the guidance in 2010. In order to reflect these changes, the 2013 Watchlisting Guidance was developed over a period of several months by an IPC under the auspices of the Presidential Policy Directive One (PPD 1) process with representatives from the Departments of State, Treasury, Defense, Justice and Homeland Security, the Office of the Director of National Intelligence, the Central Intelligence Agency, the National Security Agency, the Defense Intelligence Agency, the National Counterterrorism Center, the Federal Bureau of Investigation, and the Terrorist Screening Center. The Deputies Committee adopted the recommendation of the IPC to approve the 2013 Watchlisting Guidance on March 12, 2013.

The 2013 Watchlisting Guidance has a new structure and is organized in a way that mirrors the watchlisting cycle. It is now a single document divided as follows into fives chapters, with significant watchlisting foundational documents for reference, and a list of definitions, acronyms, and abbreviations:

- Chapter 1: Watchlisting Process and Procedures;
- Chapter 2: Minimum Identifying Criteria;
- Chapter 3: Minimum Substantive Derogatory Criteria;
- Chapter 4: No Fly, Selectee and Expanded Selectee Lists Implementation Guidance;
- Chapter 5; Encounter Management and Analysis;
- Appendix 1: Definitions;
- Appendix 2: Homeland Security Presidential Directive 6;
- Appendix 3; Memorandum of Understanding on the Integration and Use of Screening Information to Protect Against Terrorism (TSC MOD);
- Appendix 4; Addendum B to the TSC MOU;
- Appendix 5: Memorandum of Understanding between the Intelligence Community, Federal Law Enforcement Agencies, and the Department of Homeland Security Concerning Information Sharing (Information Sharing MOU);
- Appendix 6: Executive Order 13388, Further Strengthening the Sharing of Terrorism Information to Protect Americans;
- Appendix 7: Department of Justice Protocol on Terrorist Nominations;

- Appendix 8: Memorandum of Understanding on Terrorist Redress Procedures (TSC Redress MOU);
- Appendix 9: Presidential Memorandum Regarding 12/25/2009 Terrorist Attack;
- Appendix 10: Acronyms and Abbreviations;
- Appendix 11: Summary of Changes and Updates from the 2012 Watehlisting Guidance.

The 2013 Watehlisting Guidance includes the following substantive policy changes and updates:

- New, amended, or clarified definitions are included for the terms "aggregator," "derogatory information," "encounter," "enhancement," "foreign fighters," "fragmentary information," "known terrorist," "lone wolf," "operationally capable," "particularized derogatory information," "reasonable suspicion," "terrorism screening information," "terrorism and/or terrorist activities," and "U.S. Person" (Appendix 1);
- Nominators are instructed to send available information to the National Counterterrorism Center for consideration and additional review where reasonable minds could disagree on a record (Chapter 1);
- Nominating Departments and Agencies are instructed to prioritize the identification of new Known or Suspected Terrorists who meet the reasonable suspicion standard, along with the identifying and derogatory information most useful to the watchlisting and screening effort (Chapter 1);
- Nominating Agencies are to conduct periodic reviews of their nominations of U.S. Persons, at minimum on an annual basis (Chapter 1);
- Detailed instructions are described for handling U.S. Person information and ensuring that proper coordination processes are implemented (Chapters 1 and 3);
- The guidance regarding minimum identifying criteria has been revamped and exceptions clarified (Chapter 2);
- The guidance has been revised to provide Nominators with more flexibility regarding nominations of individuals based on fragmentary information (Chapter 2);
- The minimum substantive derogatory criteria guidance has been restructured to elaborate on instances of where particularized derogatory information is required to meet the reasonable suspicion standard, and when reasonable suspicion is established by other authority (Chapter 3);
- The minimum substantive derogatory criteria has been restructured to enable the watchlisting community to more clearly distinguish between watchlisting based on substantive derogatory criteria that meets the reasonable suspicion standard from watchlisting for purposes that support immigration and visa screening activities of the Department of Homeland Security and the Department of State (Chapter 3);
- Revised guidance is provided regarding the watchlisting of individuals based on information provided by a foreign government (Chapter 3);
- The guidance contains two additional categories of alien non-terrorists in the databases maintained by the National Counterterrorism Center and the Terrorist Screening Center to support immigration and visa screening activities of the Department of Homeland Security and the Department of State (e.g., individuals who have a defined relationship with the Known or Suspected Terrorist, but whose involvement with the Known or Suspected Terrorist's activities is unknown (TIDE Category Code 50) and aliens for whom additional intelligence is required (TIDE Category Code 99)) (Chapter 3);
- The Implementing Guidelines regarding the No Fly and Selectee List criteria have been updated and clarified (e.g., Guantanamo Bay detainees are now included on the No Fly List, as required

by 49 U.S.C. Section 44903(j)(2)(C)(v)) (Chapter 4);

- Use of the One Time Waiver Policy is addressed to facilitate travel under controlled conditions of certain U.S. Citizen Known or Suspected Terrorists (Chapter 4);
- The guidance reflects the creation of the Expanded Selectee List, an export to the Transportation Security Administration of Known and Suspected Terrorist records within the Terrorist Screening Database that contain a full name and complete date of birth to support airline passenger screening (Chapter 4); and
- The guidance reflects the authority of the Terrorist Screening Center Director to make individual watchlist determinations (i.e., placement on the No Fly, Selectee and Expanded Selectee Lists) during exigent circumstanccs (Chapter 4).

These changes to the Watchlisting Guidance are intended to make the watchlisting process more flexible, agile, and inclusive in order to respond to additional terrorism threats while providing the watchlisting community detailed guidance concerning the watchlisting policy of the U.S. Government.

The 2013 Watchlisting Guidance describes the U.S. Government's comprehensive watchlisting policies and process and includes Sensitive Security Information. Accordingly, Departments and Agencies who received copies of the 2013 Watchlisting Guidance are instructed to carefully control and share the guidance with only those individuals who are directly involved in the terrorist watchlisting and screening process.

Nothing in the 2013 Watchlisting Guidance is intended to restrict the authority of any Department or Agency to act as provided by law, statute, or regulation, or to restrict any Agency from enforcing any laws within its authority or jurisdiction